COLLINS *Ess*

CW01597067

Managing Your Primary Classroom

Mick Waters

Collins Educational

An imprint of HarperCollins*Publishers*

Acknowledgements

I would like to thank some people who were directly or indirectly involved in the development of this book:
Helen Nicholls for the example of school notes on display in Chapter 4.
Jenny Tyrrell for the examples of group work in Chapter 6.
Children and teachers across the country for examples of their work.

Published by Collins Educational
An imprint of HarperCollins*Publishers* Ltd
77-85 Fulham Palace Road
London W6 8JB

First published 1996

ISBN 0 00 317718 1

Illustrations by Julian Baker Illustrations and Jenny Mumford.
Designed by Chi Leung
Printed and bound by Scotprint Ltd, Musselburgh

Contents

Introduction

Nearly every primary school teacher is interested in classroom organisation and management. Teachers buy books on the subject, they go on courses and they try to find more effective ways of organising and managing their classrooms. On in-service courses, teachers often want to discuss classroom organisation and management, but any examination of issues steps directly into the centre of the teacher's working life, explores the practical realities of decision-making, and sometimes becomes uncomfortable.

There is no single recipe for good practice, no perfect solution. Classrooms are subtle, complex and complicated places. They contain different combinations of people who come together to teach and to learn in fairly artificial circumstances. However some teachers *do* achieve more than others, children in one classroom *are* different from those in another, and some teachers *are* more well organised than others.

Surveys by OFSTED constantly refer to the importance of effective management in the classroom. Effective classroom organisation depends on a sound educational philosophy, and a set of sound educational principles. As these principles move into practice, teachers often become defensive and unwilling to accept the challenge associated with effective organisation. Arguments often appear to be about trivialities when in fact they are about the very essence of classroom life, which leads to sound organisation and teaching towards a philosophy.

This book addresses the detail of effective classroom organisation. Whether you are a experienced teacher, new to the profession, a supply teacher or a student in training, this book gives practical suggestions on how to make the classroom work for teachers and children. There are examples to help get things started and checklists to make sure they are happening. Many primary teachers already do a lot of the things mentioned in this book, but if you look for the ideas that are new to you and try them in your classroom, new possibilities will unfold.

1 The classroom - why change it?

Why look again at the classroom? Why spend time trying to reorganise it and do things better, especially since it will never be perfect? Here are several very good reasons for making a start:

1 Survival

The job of teaching is becoming more complex and demanding. If the classroom can be organised more effectively in physical terms for maximum efficiency, then the teacher is more likely to survive the day in an even temper, remain unflustered, and feel less tired.

2 More effective performance

If the classroom is organised efficiently then the teacher is able to perform more effectively because things that are needed are to hand, everyone works together better, and the expectations of the curriculum can be more easily achieved. Effectiveness is the domain not only of the teacher but also of the children; in well organised classrooms there is a greater opportunity for children to work effectively.

3 Greater confidence

If the classroom is organised then both teacher and children can be confident that things will work.

4 Manageable work load

If the teacher is not worried about the organisation of the details of the classroom, other aspects of work become easier to handle. As a result the curriculum content and the needs of individual children become the focus of thinking, rather than retrieval of resources, planning of furniture and dealing with breakdowns in organisation.

5 More flexibility

If classroom conditions are well planned there is greater scope for using different patterns of organisation and work to fit individual sessions. Since a considerable proportion of the organisation can be taken for granted, special events can be focused upon.

6 Less stress

In the organised classroom, where people feel confident, the work load is manageable, the performances of children and teachers are effective and the focus has gone beyond survival into a more flexible, composed situation, there is less stress for both teacher and children.

2 Successful classrooms

Some classrooms are more successful than others and there are some essential features which can help to distinguish quality within them. What makes some classrooms work better than others?

High expectations
Classrooms that are going to be successful give an impression that high quality achievement is expected. Children and teachers know what is expected and they communicate this in all sorts of ways. Teachers make children believe they can achieve and children in turn approach their activities with a positive regard, anticipating success.

A production emphasis
In quality classrooms things get done. These are the classes where children achieve a greater quantity of work than in others, and in less time. This can be due to the expectation that things are going to be produced. On the part of the teacher this means saying to the children, '*You have so long to complete this task*'. In turn, children set themselves deadlines that can be met. However, children should not be limited so they work at an unreal speed or produce shoddy, half-hearted work. For children to produce an art work gem, they may need to be involved in detailed, concentrated work over a long period.

Children should be clear about what they are trying to do, and any anticipation of allowing time to drift away should be discouraged. Even when they are working in groups there should be an expected time limit and production emphasis. The group or the individual may fail to achieve what was anticipated, but given a time limit, children should be able to say why their plans have not materialised. In good classrooms children are able to say what represents success.

An efficient 'workshop' approach
Successful classrooms demonstrate an efficient workshop attitude. They are tidy, organised, well disciplined and, while comfortable and stimulating, are highly efficient. People know what they are doing, and why they are doing it. They know where things are kept and who is responsible for what, and they take responsibilities, understanding why these responsibilities are given.

Rigorous work behaviour
In successful classrooms people work rigorously. They are organised in their work, efficient, productive and have high expectations. This applies to both teachers and pupils. The teacher's desk is organised, orderly and tidy and, when it sometimes becomes confused, efforts are

made to bring it back to order. Likewise, the children's desks or work places. Pupils work with a realistic level of noise, with consideration for each other and for themselves, in that they use the time at their disposal as effectively as possible. In a one-hour session, time wasted is kept to a minimum so that the sixty minutes available are used to good effect.

Pupil involvement and awareness
All these aspects of successful classrooms rely on the involvement of pupils and their heightened awareness of what is going on in the room in which they are intended to learn. In successful classrooms:

- the pupils are involved in making decisions about the way in which the classroom should be organised and run. Being involved helps them to be aware of why decisions are made but they are also aware of decisions that are made for their own good that have not necessarily involved them
- the pupils recognise that they have responsibilities and that the teacher has the overall responsibility
- the teacher is concerned to offer children levels of responsibility and that the children take the responsibility offered and use it effectively
- the teacher is quick to point out where pupils are not reaching the high expectations of responsibility that are offered.

These features naturally overlap and intertwine. Nevertheless, it is possible to sense the degree to which a classroom is successful within these criteria. In some classrooms children can be seen working effectively and efficiently and with a high degree of success to produce quality work. In others the picture is less encouraging.

3 *What types of work go on in the classroom?*

As a result of the development of the National Curriculum, 5-14 Guidelines and OFSTED there is a constant emphasis upon subjects. Children are described as doing English, mathematics, science, IT, and so on. Sometimes they move into sand and water play, construction, or the imaginative play area, but the conversation is usually about the content of the work in which children are engaged.

Types of work for children

The work that children do could be looked at in a slightly different way, moving away from the subject matter. It could be classified under the following sorts of headings:

- Completing
- Novel
- Self-selecting
- Continuing unaided
- Challenge
- Teacher-directed route through selected activities.
- Routine and practice
- Sharing skills

These ways of looking at types of work have implications for organisation. The child completing or continuing work unaided should not need the teacher available or present. Similarly, the child doing routine practice work should not need the teacher. The child on a teacher-directed route, for example through a mathematics scheme, may need a teacher infrequently, to suggest ways forward or for an explanation. The child on a novel piece of learning or a challenge may need the teacher for a considerable amount of time. To address the problems of trying to run the complex classroom, teachers need to consider the types of work in which children are engaged, apart from its content or subject, to identify which demand more teacher attention.

Teacher input

There are a number of aspects to each task which will determine how much teacher input is required. Each aspect is a continuum. The style of the activity and the experience of the children will determine the level of input and where on each continuum you are. A realistic balance of activities is needed to ensure your input is available when and where necessary and is manageable.

Active .... Passive
Open-ended .... Closed
Using skills already acquired .... New skills
Collaborative .... Individual
Simple .... Complex

Short-term .... Extended
Structured .... Flexible
Routine .... Novel
Teacher-independent .... Teacher-dependent

It is important when planning work in the classroom to consider:

1 What sort of work children are going to be involved in?
2 Which aspects will enable children to work alone without needing the teacher to support, oversee, challenge or direct?

Levels of provision

Another way of looking at the types of work for children is to look at the levels of provision needed for different sorts of work:

- Clerical - so much work is writing and reading.
- Wet - when it is wet work, messy time, decisions must be made about how many at once and where in the room.
- Untidy - how many, when, and if it is something that is going to take a while, what about storage?
- Noisy - at times it is necessary to organise for noise. Where, when, and how many children can take part and what are the others going to do?
- Concentrated - some work demands absolute concentration and might be better done away from the noise and bustle that comes with some of the other tasks!
- Plugged-in - work at the sink, the computer, the TV or tape recorder. Since such work can only be done in a particular area, usually not everyone can do the task at once. So what about the rest? Do they need some routine, teacher independent work?

If you think about the types of work you are providing for the children and go beyond the simple subject classification, it is easier to understand why the primary classroom is such a complicated place. Whole class teaching can take place, but other dimensions at different times must be planned for.

To begin the process of organising the classroom it might be helpful to work through the questions on the chart on pages 10-11, which will help to justify your chosen organisation solution. The reasons behind your answers are as important as the answers themselves. There could be lots more questions but these raise the issues of:

- the types of work children do
- how much they work as a class, a group, or individually
- what the teacher's role is
- what sorts of spaces need to be created in the classroom.

Whether you work in a large room or small room, a team-teaching situation, a bay with shared areas, or a mobile, you need to think through the questions and be sure of your reasons.

Question	Yes/No	Reason
1 Do you want to address the whole class briefly at the beginning, end and during lessons?		
2 Do you want to spend at least some 15 minutes sessions addressing the whole class with explanation, instruction or question?		
3 Do you want to write on a board for everyone to read?		
4 Do you want children to work alone for at least 20 minute sessions?		
5 Do you want children to work together in pairs for 20 minutes 30 minutes 40 minutes		
6 Do you want children to work together in bigger groups?		
7 Do you want to limit the number of children working at once on: Reading Writing Discussion Maths (books) Maths activity Experiments Art IT Listening to teacher Play		
8 Do you want children to work without the teacher? Reading Writing Discussion Maths (books) Maths activity Experiments Art IT Listening to teacher Play		

Question	Yes/No	Reason
9 Do you want to gather children together?		
10 Do you want to engage the children in discussion as a class?		
11 Do you want to 'lead' children in activity such as poems, choral speaking, songs, timetables, spelling?		
12 Do you want children to have a basic set of equipment?		
13 Do you want children to sort out equipment for themselves for various activities? Reading Writing Discussion Maths (books) Maths activity Experiments Art IT Listening to teacher Play		
14 Do you want children to plan their use of time? All +50% -50% very little none		

4 Arranging the room - eight steps to success

How the classroom should be organised depends on what is seen as important. Although there is no simple formula, it is possible to work through a set of stages when planning and organising the arrangement of space in the classroom. Any action taken will be influenced by the overall philosophy of how learning should take place, the teaching style that is to be adopted, and the need to minimise disruption as well as maximise opportunities for effective teaching and learning.

Step 1 - Establish a focal point

It is essential when looking at the way the classroom is arranged to establish the place from which the teacher is to make announcements, give instructions, offer explanations, give feedback to children and take questions. This will be the focal point of the classroom. In some classrooms this might be in front of the chalkboard, which is then available for notes, illustrations or demonstrations. The teacher might have a second focal point, for use when the children are working in a dispersed way around the classroom, sitting at desks, or working at benches or easels. A focal point can also exist where the children are gathered. If there is a large enough carpet for the children to meet on at the beginning or end of sessions then the teacher might need a focal point, such as the teacher's chair, from which to make announcements.

Wherever the focal point is, the teacher must try to adopt the discipline of consistently offering announcements from the focal point and resisting making general comments from anywhere else. The position of the focal point does not need to be made apparent to the children, though there is no harm in doing so, but children will give status to announcements from a particular place.

Most primary school teachers move around the classroom. If a teacher is in the habit of working with a group on a particular problem in the far corner of the room, but looking up to make an announcement to everybody, it would appear that the announcement does not have the status that it would if the teacher moved back to the focal point to make it. This is extremely important because to set high expectations and establish rigorous work behaviour, there must be discipline in the way that information is offered - a focal point can create that disciplined environment.

Many teachers have a confusion of focal points. They have the teacher's desk at which they sit to make an announcement. They sometimes sit on the front of the desk in order to talk to the children and then move to a chalkboard. They then make announcements from various parts of the room as they move around. The value of this is extremely limited and it is much more effective for teacher announcements to come from a consistent focal point.

Choosing a focal point

1 All the children need to be able to see without obstruction. The classroom should be arranged so that no child has their back to the person making the announcements or needs to move their chair to be able to see.

2 The most effective focal points are placed away from windows and have a background which is a solid wall rather than curtaining. Apart from the possible distraction that occurs when standing in front of a window, many viewers will see only a silhouette or outline shape of the person speaking. Since much information comes from facial clues it is important that these can be seen. A wall offers resonance of sound and clarity of message in a way that a curtain does not. Curtains deaden sound; walls are much more likely to vibrate the sound around the room. These simple points have an important impact on the effectiveness of the focal point.

Step 2 - Create working alcoves

For many years teachers have tried to break down the box shape of their classroom in order to offer children more intimate and pleasant surroundings. This is very worthwhile but, in creating alcoves or bays, certain principles have to be considered.

Research in commercial settings suggests that office workers in open-plan buildings establish their own zones by using filing cabinets, cupboards and shelving units, both to make a private area and to reduce visual distraction. It is now thought that in classrooms children are distracted not so much by the noise of others as by interruptions to their visual concentration.

Breaking down the classroom into smaller alcoves, by moving cupboards, display racks and storage cabinets, creates a more intimate atmosphere and also reduces the visual distraction across the classroom. Children feel they are not in a 'big' classroom and the teacher can work with a small group in an 'isolated' part of the room. Different activities can take place and the classroom will feel 'zoned'.

There will always be times, however when the teacher needs to talk to everyone; to use the focal point. In some classrooms the need to establish intimacy and group opportunities has been given more importance than the need of the teacher to speak to the whole class. Even this second step involves a compromise of ideals. Although numerous small alcoves may be desirable, visibility should take priority.

Step 3 - Establish busy and browsing areas

The working alcoves can contain activity. Most teachers have areas or bays which have a direct subject focus. Nearly every classroom has a reading area and many now have writing corners, art areas, IT areas, messy areas and wet areas. However, some teachers then struggle because they are unclear in their own minds, and cannot communicate to children, exactly what these areas are for.

It must be established whether the area is for browsing or being busy in. If it is a busy area, the child goes there to do the work associated with that subject. If it is for browsing, the child selects appropriate apparatus and brings it back to a suitable place to do the work.

In infant classrooms, children tend to go to the play area to play, the art area to do art, and the reading area to read. As children get older and physically bigger, the amount of space available in classrooms tends to reduce, and as they learn to write children spend more and more time in clerical activity. Thus in most classrooms there is a lot of furniture intended as writing places for most of the time. Other parts of the room become areas from which resources are collected rather than areas in which to work. They become browsing rather than busy areas.

It is not very important whether children work in the browsing areas or whether they just go there to select materials; what matters is that everybody knows and understands the purpose of the areas. It may be better to use these areas as storage places rather than pupils working under inadequate conditions in the designated zones.

There are principles that underline the efficiency of browsing and busy areas. The ground rules need to be clearly established:

- How many children are allowed to be there at once?
- Are they allowed to leave their work in progress out or do they have to put it away every time they reach their time limit?
- How is absolute tidiness ensured?
- How can the teacher make sure that pupils play a full part in maintaining the order of the area?

It is easy in theory to allocate monitors to each area. However, this can lead children to think that responsibility lies with someone else and that tidiness is not a general concern.

Step 4 - Organise resources and storage

Materials and equipment

One reason that many classrooms are limited for space is that too much is kept in them. To make maximum use of space teachers should store only what is needed and not what might come in handy one day. To operate a whole school approach properly, central storage must be found for many of the consumable items and a skip for the rest.

Cast an eye around your classroom, and think how long it is since you last used some of the equipment there. Anything that has not been used for, say, five years can be discarded to create a bit more space. This applies also to reading books that nobody reads, textbooks that nobody uses any more and art equipment that has had its day. It also means you can throw away much of that junk. Do you really need so many yoghurt pots, toilet roll tubes and egg cartons? Unless these materials are used on a regular basis, perhaps it would be better to collect them when they are needed.

Within the classroom it is essential to have a 'teacher-only' area for equipment that is not available to the children. This area should be well organised. Tidiness and organisation cannot be expected from children if teachers exhibit other characteristics!

However the space is used in the classroom, it has to be used logically. There should be reasons why things are kept where they are, and in most cases resources and equipment should be stored where they are needed. Storage is a matter of logistics and careful thought will yield the most efficient access to resources. This in turn will develop the most disciplined and rigorous classroom.

If storage is logical then it can be explained, and the explanation should be offered to children so that they can see that it is in their best interest to maintain the systems that have been set up. Again the teacher is responsible for organising the classroom but that responsibility has to be taken to some extent by the children.

Monitors can be self-defeating within the classroom. It is very easy to try to maintain systems of resource organisation and storage by appointing monitors and putting up lists to ensure that all the jobs get done. In so many classes where monitors operate, the overall standard is very lax except for the various times when the monitors have their purge and put things back to rights. For high expectations, rigorous attitudes to learning and a calm and efficient classroom it is better to keep things right all the time, and the best way to do that is for everybody to take responsibility.

Work in progress

The storage of work in progress poses a significant problem, but children can be helped to maintain an efficient workshop within the classroom. Start where the children keep their own materials and belongings. Whether they are in a locker, a cabinet full of drawers or a tray under the desk, it is reasonable to expect children to keep their belongings tidy. However, they will not do this by magic. They need to be shown how to organise, how to keep things tidy and why certain things are stored in some ways rather than in others. This is an area where, if children are left to explore and discover, they are likely to become very disheartened, when in fact a little time spent showing them now and again would help them to achieve results.

Untidy lockers mean that children's work gets messy and dog-eared and pride is lost. Tidy lockers mean that there is a chance that their work will maintain its status for a while. There are those who believe that the child's locker is private property and that the teacher is breaking some confidence by peeking inside it. Even so, there is no harm in showing children how big books fit below small books, how rulers and pencils go down the side and not between books and how to ensure that not too much is kept in one place. Children need help in most things: only with help can they take responsibility.

Some work in progress is difficult to store, for example pieces of writing which have to go through various drafts before they reach the finished product. Teachers come up with ingenious solutions for such problems; one rather nice one is to staple two envelope wallet files back to back, and in one side to keep finished products, pieces of work that have been displayed, and pieces of work that are particularly well presented. In the other side notes, drafts and scribbles can be kept, but now and again cleared out because they are no longer needed. However, a selection of drafts sometimes needs to be kept for parents' evenings.

Part of the teacher-only area needs to be kept clear for the storage of such things as models and half-finished experiments. Too often children lose heart because somebody damages the model that they were making. To avoid this in an overcrowded classroom, with children trying to use minimal resources to maximum effect, keep part-finished work in a particular area.

Children also need to understand clearly the use of such things as:

- computer disks - where they are kept, how they are stored, that they go back into their wallets
- calculators - what you do when the batteries run out, where the batteries are kept
- paintbrushes - how they are stored, where they are stored, what they are stored with.

The overall maintenance of the classroom thus becomes the responsibility of the children instead of the teacher.

Labelling drawers

When you are next in a classroom with labels on the drawers, open the one saying 'rulers'. If it really contains rulers then the system is working. If it contains three pairs of scissors, two protractors and a button then in fact the word 'rulers' is a code word for 'jumble'. If you put labels on drawers then you must be absolutely vigilant about ensuring that the drawer contains what it is supposed to.

Instead of having labels that are ignored because they become part of the furniture, think of other ways of organising materials. You could place the drawers in their rack and have a chart which indicates what is kept in each drawer on the basis of co-ordinates within the rack, so that the drawer becomes the numbered co-ordinate. Scissors are kept in drawer 4:2; four across and two down. Imaginative use of the classroom is one way to encourage children to use aspects of maths for a purpose.

Pencils, rubbers and rulers

The organisation of resources in the classroom is fundamental to children's success in learning, and in the end it comes down to what many people see as trivial detail. For instance, how do you organise the pencils when there are 32 children in the classroom? You could:

- have 32 pencils in one locker or in a box somewhere in the classroom
- put some pencils in a tin on each of the tables where children sit
- give the children one pencil each for which they are responsible.

Each of those three options has implications. If you have 32 pencils in a box somewhere in the classroom, whenever they are needed there is likely to be a crowd pushing to get a pencil. Crowds, lines and queues create some major behaviour problems in classrooms.

How about a small number of pencils in a tin on each table? This implies that children have responsibility for the tinful, but also indicates no individual responsibility, so the child may think, 'if I lose my pencil I can get another one from the tin,' and since there is a group responsibility the group eventually finds itself short of pencils and accepts the consequences.

If each child has its own pencil it encourages responsibility but some children are going to lose theirs, and the consequences of loss must be carefully thought out, because deceit may become part of classroom life. If losing a pencil is a major issue, the first thought of anybody unable to find theirs is to take someone else's. Names can be put on pencils or the end of the pencil can be shaved and the name written along the barrel, but in practice this encourages longer-named individuals to take a shorter-named pencil, shave off the name and add their own. The child with the shortest name has a big problem when they lose their pencil or have it stolen! Systems are needed to ensure that children often check where pencils are, especially in classrooms where children work in different places for different activities.

Perhaps an easier way than any of these is to give each child one brand new pencil at the start of each half term. Insist that there will be no names on the pencils, if they are lost there will be no fuss, no time spent looking for them, and there are spare pencils available to hurry the learning along. At the end of each half term all the old pencils are collected, and new ones are distributed. Although this

…pensive consider the cost of paint washed down the sink, dried …es, computers standing idle while class enquiries on lost pencils …tinue, then perhaps the cost of six pencils a year per child is not enormous. If hundreds of minutes of teaching time are saved then cost effectiveness could be important.

Step 5 - Plan display

Display has to be carefully planned and organised. If it is planned from the beginning it has a greater chance of being successful. Displays can perform many functions but they should answer one of three questions:

Whose is it?
Encourage some notion of ownership and celebrate children's achievements.

What is it?
Develop the sense of the curious.

Isn't it ...?
Develop the sense of appreciation. It could be good, amazing, ugly, confusing. It does not matter what it 'isn't', but 'Isn't it ...?' is a wonderful question for children to ask.

The next question to be answered is: *Why is this particular display being displayed?:*

- Does it help children's learning?
- Does it help them to understand what learning is about?
- Does it help to move their learning forward?

It is also important to consider how long to keep a display. Is it still relevant, stimulating, tidy? Too often the function of display is simply to make the classroom look nice, forgetting that looking nice is only part of the answer. Working for the wall, and the instant display to satisfy the outsiders who want to look around, must be abandoned.

Classroom displays should challenge children's thinking, stimulate their learning and show sensitivity and concern about what they achieve. It is important that display is managed as efficiently as possible. The use of templates, drapes, frames and stands makes effective display a quicker process. A central store in the school increases choice for teachers. It need not only be teachers, though. Display can be organised by classroom assistants, parents or children as long as everyone understands the principles.

It is possible to offer guidelines that can be very easily managed and that can create a set of precepts for teachers, so that the approaches taken within a school are compatible. One school produces helpful hints on 'effective display' on one side of A3 paper *(see pages 20-21)*. Read them through and compare them with the advice given in your school. Use the ideas as a basis for discussion with the people concerned and then watch them help to transform the room!

Step 6 - Review traffic areas

The ability to move around easily reduces tension and cuts down problems in the classroom. Picture the little infant coming to show the teacher a lovely model made in Lego. She trips over the outstretched legs of a child lying on the floor painting, she tumbles, and the Lego lands in the pottery being done by two children not a metre away. If only traffic areas were constantly free so that children could move around without falling over or bumping into each other!

If children keep their belongings close to where they are expected to sit, their need to cross paths as they move around the classroom is limited. This level of detail in logistical planning is very desirable because if children are less likely to collide the teacher is more relaxed, which in itself will lead to a more positive learning situation.

Step 7 - Establish a standards zone outside

Many teachers think that organising the classroom means organising what goes on from their doorway inwards. But to set high expectations and rigorous work behaviour the best place to start is in the corridor or as children enter the work space. The aim is to set a standards zone which foreshadows expectations in the classroom.

Take a wander outside your classroom. Is it a cloakroom strewn with coats fallen from hooks, plastic bags and various heaps of old paper and cardboard boxes? Or is it a statement of what you would like to see in the classroom: organised, tidy and efficient?

Traffic areas can be organised in cloakrooms so that children coming from the classroom are not all crowded around the same pegs:

- Can children's coats be spread around the pegs so that crowding, and consequently problem behaviour, is minimised?
- Can children's work be displayed in the cloakroom area following its display in the classroom, so that other pupils can see it?
- Can displays be borrowed from other classrooms to show the sort of work going on elsewhere in the school?

Whatever the means, the aim is to promote the quality anticipated within your classroom as far away from the actual classroom as possible.

Step 8 - Explain

No system works unless it is carefully explained. Systems need explaining beforehand and while they are in use. For children you need to explain very clearly how the classroom operates. If children are to take real responsibility then they need to understand why this responsibility is to be taken, and the thinking behind the ground rules

Preparing the boards before the work

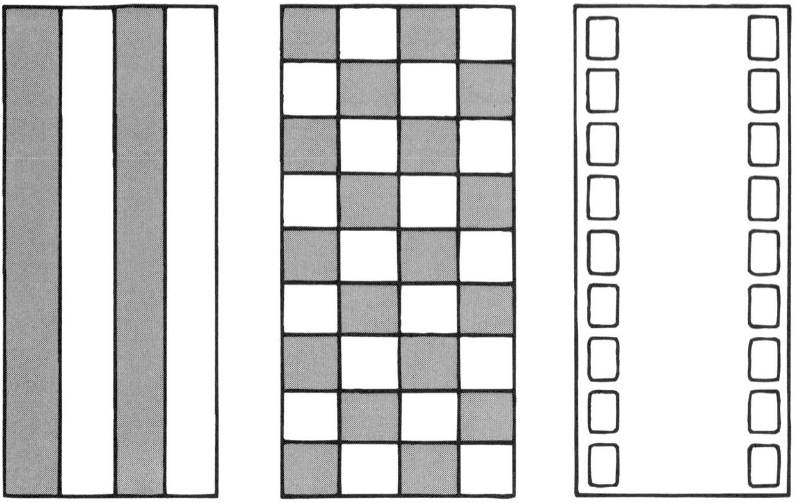

Stipes Checks Film strips

DISPLAY

..... Quick tips .... Helpful hints .....

- Letterbank
- Stencils
- Scripts Book
- Photocopier-enlarge, reduce

- Prepared/ mounted labels
- Single mounted
- Double mounted
- Triple mounted
- 'Ed print'

- Stuffed/ padded letters
- Shadow lettering
- Hang it on the line
- Hanging letters

- Covered boxes
- Twigs
- Bricks
- Pebbles

• *Parents* • *Art/Display Club* • *Classroom assistants*

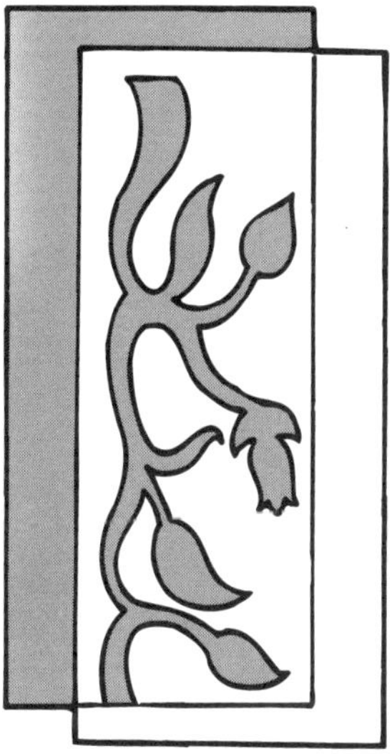

Cutting through

- Finger painting
- Sponging
- Printing
- Drawing on to O,H,P and projecting on to board.
- Building out 3D layers using boxes.
- Traditional frieze (drawing/ collage)

Basic rule

Prepare board,
artefacts,
plant,
drape,

Explanations
Questions

Plan it first !

Creating depth by fixing and joining

boxes for building out

cup hooks

toilet rolls for levels

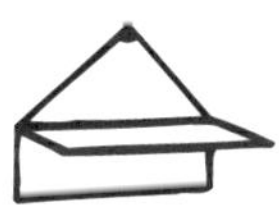

use boxes to build shelves

Tools

- papers
- pens
- staple remover
- cup hooks
- fishing line
- string
- knife
- scissors
- staple gun
- hand stapler
- ruler

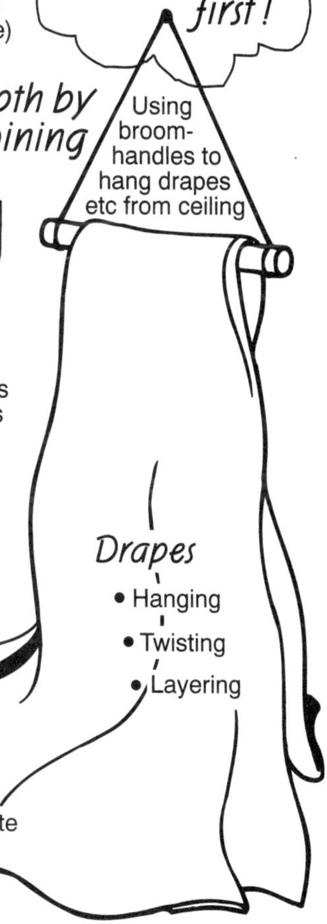

Using broom-handles to hang drapes etc from ceiling

Drapes

- Hanging
- Twisting
- Layering

Building environments with stockingette

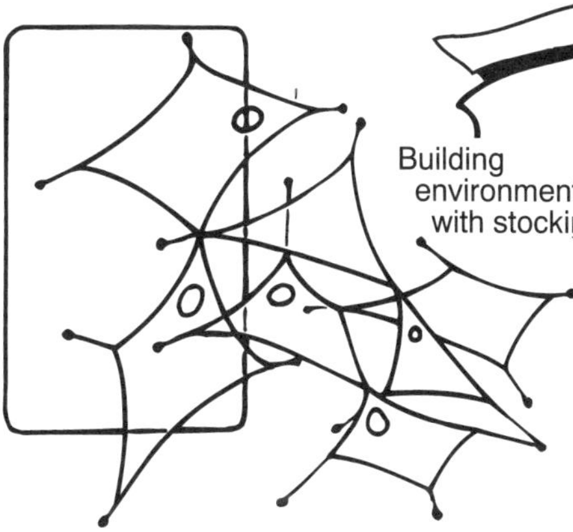

Environments

- *Stimulus:* inspiration
- *Interactive:* something to do
- *Reflective:* sharing
- *On going:* work in progress

in the classroom. So when it comes to explaining, there are some important things to remember:

- Tell them *where* things are
- Tell them *how* to use things
- Tell them *when* to use things
- Tell them *who* can use things
- Tell them *why* things are kept where they are
- Say 'thank you' when they do things well.

Routines

If you are trying to set up and explain routines, then they need to be properly thought through. Much of classroom life is about routines; once these are established then many disturbances and problems recede.

- Explain and justify
- Practise
- Praise
- Reinforce, explain and justify
- Say 'thank you'.

Some routines need to be talked about until you are 'blue in the face':

- Resources
- Work levels
- Self-organisation
- Out-of-class image

and remember, plenty of praise and thanks.

Some routines are obvious and can become principles for the classroom. However, because these are obvious to adults, teachers sometimes imagine that they are obvious to children. Some of the simplest things must be reiterated to children throughout the primary school to help them be effective and to produce quality work:

- Sit properly on the chair
- Organise the table or the work surface efficiently and effectively
- Talk; don't gossip
- Spend time, don't waste it.

The effective teacher explains all these things to the children over and over again. They become the basis of how the classroom operates effectively. They are explained at times of calm, not when things are going wrong. Children are told why the classroom is organised as it is and helped to see how their classroom works. They are taken through the eight steps to success so that they, in turn, can succeed.

You might like to think how you would explain the eight steps taken to achieve success in your own teaching situation. In the example on pages 23-24, a teacher explains how her Year 2 unit for two classes is organised by her and her colleague. As you read it reflect on the way she brings in the aspects covered in this chapter. How would you describe your own organisation to someone else?

Classroom organisation

In order to make full use of the available space and resources, I organised the classroom into separate working areas which could be shared by all the children. The classroom was sub-divided into three areas by partitioned doors which at the moment are always kept open. In the first area is a carpeted bay with seating (benches, bean bags) where a group, a class or all of Y2 could gather for discussion. Adjoining this area is a large reading corner where books are displayed and seating provided to create a cosy, quiet place for reading or for listening to story or poetry tapes. Next to this bay is a wet area with two sink units and two large laminated tables. This serves as an area for all art work and the relevant materials and equipment are stored here and made easily accessible for the children to use. In the centre of the room are four groups of tables each seating up to six children. Each table is equipped with pencils, rubbers, sharpeners, crayons (wax and pencil), felt tips and rulers. This eliminates unnecessary time in finding these essentials. This area is used mainly for language or topic work.

The second area is used as a technology area. There are two computers with concept keyboards and printers. Equipment including saws, hammers, blocks and materials (card, wood, junk, fabric) necessary for making models, sewing and experimenting are readily available in this area and are conveniently stored and labelled. The constructional toys, games, jigsaws are also kept here and there is a large carpeted area which provides space for imaginative play. This term, one corner has become an 'Underwater world'; because of a water topic. It is a stimulating area which encourages the children to dress up and let fantasy emerge. This area is restricted to four children and is used as part of a structured play situation.

Lastly, the third area is equipped for science and mathematics. It also has four groups of tables which sit up to six children and are similarly equipped as the other tables. There is a carpeted area used for discussion purposes and a wet area with one sink used for scientific experiments, volume and quantity work. Mathematical and scientific equipment, books and resources are centrally stored here.

Outside are sand and water trays and an animals enclosure with rabbits and guinea pigs. Throughout the areas are horizontal and vertical surfaces used for displaying children's work or as a display of stimulating artefacts around a topic of current concern, or as an active display encouraging participation. There is no separate stock room or cupboard as I thought it would take up valuable space and I prefer to store the resources in places where they are readily available in clearly labelled drawers, trays or cupboards for the children to select and use.

Grouping for learning

The children are initially grouped into two classes and allocated a teacher. These groups remain constant for administrative and registration purposes, parent interviews, management of 'reading' books and certain other timetabled activities, e.g. library, swimming. However the children are further grouped across the two classes with one of eight colour groups. The children are grouped according to varying factors including age, friendship, ability, sex, etc. These groups do sometimes change according to the task or social interactions.

After morning registration and welcome, all Y2 children meet together in one of the carpeted bays. From here four groups are selected, according to the task or learning experiences, to work with one of the teachers in one of the areas. The teacher then organises the work for the children according to the area they are to work in that morning,
e.g. Area 1 - language/art/topic Area 2 - technology/play
Area 3 - science/mathematics.

The teacher is responsible for differentiating the tasks according to the children and to organise resources and management of groups. The children usually exchange working areas and teachers when there is a natural break, i.e. after playtimes, as we find these working sessions are long enough. However, if additional time with the same group is needed we can be flexible.

Changing areas after playtimes also eliminates time wasting and excess movement. My colleague and I also make sure that the children do not associate us with certain subjects so we make sure we teach all the areas of the curriculum and work equally in all areas. However, we are also able to use each other's specialised expertise in areas such as music and art for example, whereby we take both classes for these activities at different times. This helps to ensure both breadth and balance in the curriculum.

To work successfully in this way, curriculum planning and methods of delivery and presentation have to be discussed and written up in detail. My colleague and I also meet briefly after school each day to reflect and assess the day that has gone and to organise and plan the next day's activities. However as the planning is shared the workload is halved.

This co-operative approach also makes moderation and assessment a more manageable goal, as sharing views about children's work between colleagues rapidly improves the moderation process and leads towards common understanding of achievement levels. We also aim to share the individual responsibility of discipline and it is always a pleasure to share the children's 'good work' with other adults.

5 Instructions, explanations and questions

There is a general assumption that the one thing that teachers do not need to think about is the skill of instruction and explanation - they do it nearly all the time, so they must be good at it. It is true that most teachers can give good instructions most of the time, but it is an area that needs constant development. It is relatively easy to get into a rut and give instructions in the same way all the time and to miss some of the options that are available. The skill of talking to a class group improves with practice and confidence, and whereas it was the main method of teaching a generation ago, the flexible running of a classroom means that teachers in primary schools address the class less and get less practice.

Different children can cope with different amounts of instruction or explanation. The teacher needs to decide how much at one time. Explanation can be phased over a series of lessons or instructions repeated in different ways. Some simple techniques will help the planning.

Children nowadays are more sophisticated in the way they receive communication. Through the media, children are offered highly effective, carefully structured explanations, instructions and announcements, often using resource back-up that schools will never be able to match, and a range of actions that are skilfully chosen by the media professionals. The teacher, therefore, has got to use the basic skills of instruction well to achieve the best possible results within the classroom setting.

Headlines and detail
Good announcers offer the headlines before they go into detail. This guides the listener through the message to come: it sets the agenda. It is a bit like the news on TV.

'In this lesson I am going to show you:
1 *how to create a simple screen print design*
2 *how to print the design*
3 *how to remove the paint*
4 *how to store your prints as they are produced*
5 *how to clean your materials.*
Five points in the whole process, so, let's begin with number one: how to create a simple design.'

When to clarify

Instructions sometimes require clarification and it is vital that thought is given beforehand as to which parts of the explanation will need further emphasis. It may be necessary to reinforce explanation as a result of reaction from the group, but there are some elements that can be anticipated. The choice of method for clarification is what makes one explanation different from another.

Chat groups

To stop at particular points and offer the children a chance to chat in twos or threes about what has been said will result in greater understanding. The children can:

- consider what has been said
- ask each other questions
- talk about what they do not understand
- ask the teacher questions.

Misunderstandings can often be avoided if the children are able to talk about their concerns rather than wait until the end when they have got completely lost. Children are much more likely to admit problems and less likely to try to 'cheat'.

Stage by stage to the end

Many explanations or instructions are best offered as a series, one at a time to the end. At each stage it is possible to check for understanding through talk or by asking the children to do a relevant task. This may involve demonstration, perhaps repeated with chat groups before the children attempt their effort. If it is a model that is being made, or a new technique that is being learned, the children could work in pairs, with one doing and the other watching to check for accuracy. At each stage the composite picture is built up towards the final stage. It is necessary to repeat the process fairly soon, giving lots of opportunity for practice to ensure familiarity.

Review stages

If some explanations or instructions are offered in stages, then a progress review should be built into the plan. Each stage might be reviewed, looking back through the agenda. The group could be reminded of the progress they are making by going through their agenda. The group might practise the stages so far as they reach each new one. Whatever the method, the possibilities for review and reinforcement must be thought through at the planning stage so that children can see where they are going.

Here's one I did earlier

If you are going stage by stage, then an example of each stage is helpful. A lot of preparation is needed, however, because the teacher has to make an example for each stage before the explanation begins.

Spare equipment

The examples become useful when it is necessary to use spare equipment. If the whole class, or one group, is following a series of instructions it is a good idea to have spare equipment to hand. The teacher can simply pass the struggler the spare scissors, the paper folded to stage three and carry on.

New ideas for old

One way of explaining things is to start afresh, to tell the children that the class is going to try to sort out their ideas on a topic or technique and to clarify the correct approach. Ask the children to work in small groups and list the things they know, or think important, about the topic. Then deal with the suggestions or offer a 'correct' explanation and invite the children to compare it with their suggestions.

The better teachers are at giving instructions and offering explanations, the better the classroom runs and the more success the children have.

Questions matter

Questions are a major part of classroom life and learning. However, they can be used effectively to extend or reinforce children's knowledge. Look at the issues to do with these questions and think about the possibilities:

- How often is the range of question styles used?
- When is it appropriate to use the different sorts?
- Which children need which sorts of questions?

Question strings creating thought paths

So, the old man couldn't pull up the turnip. Who helped?

Then who?

Then who?

Checking understanding - retreading

Have you noticed the pattern when we count on in 5s?

What should happen when we add blue paint to this red?

Quickfire ... flashcards ... group response

help

teacher

when

school

Right or wrong

What is the capital of Peru?

4x3?

Discussion questions

What should we do about keeping the play area tidy?

Why do you think the old lady was unhappy?

Rhetorical questions

What do we do with dirty water when we are painting?

Where do we put the Multilink?

Questions can fulfil many functions in the classroom. The teacher can accept, clarify, rephrase what is said, correct misapprehension, and lead towards explanation through questioning. The children need to know the agenda. They need to know how the questions are being used and what the response to the answer might be. If children know they are being invited to suggest reasons they react differently than if they are going to be right or wrong.

Using questions with children

Questioning can be developed in all sorts of ways; not just by the teacher asking questions out loud. The key is to develop questioning in the children. Here is an idea to try.

A teacher had a box delivered to the classroom, inside which was a new CD player which was going to be used by anyone in the school. Instead of opening it, the teacher put the box on the floor in the centre of an enormous piece of paper on which she wrote *'What is in the box?'*. By break time the paper was covered with suggestions; a few are shown here.

What is in the box?

I ricitatili

a gold staR

is it a rabts

its a sprs for boys and girls

ch33TTTs4s4

sm bucs

presnts.

Look at the range of writing, look at the assessment possibilities, look at the way some children are using full sentences and question marks, and are attempting to write what may be seen as difficult words.

All that is needed to do this is:

1 something to ask a question about, and
2 someone from outside the classroom who does not appear to know the answer to the question being asked.

On many occasions when the teacher asks a question, children must wonder why it is being asked when everyone is aware that the teacher knows the answer. This is when someone from outside is needed. In one school the midday supervisor for the class happened to be indoors because it was a wet day. Before she went home she left a question herself. During the morning the children had been working on fairy stories that had become pantomimes. Her question was, '*Which is your favourite pantomime?*' and the next day she was greeted with many, many answers. She left another question: '*Why?*'.

Leaving questions is a lovely idea because:

- it takes very little time
- it becomes a normal part of the routine of the classroom
- no child is wrong
- every child's effort is valued
- children read each others' answers
- even the weakest child will have a go
- parents can see the range of ability within the classroom when they attend the parents' evening.

To engage children in real questions and answers and to have a real purpose for writing, it is sometimes possible to use an outsider who does not know the class as a catalyst. If your appetite is whetted, just look carefully at the work in a classroom to get it going. Teachers can swap classes, lunch-time supervisors, student teachers, heads and deputies could be used, even individual children moving between classes could leave questions as they go.

6 *Effective groupwork*

What is meant by a 'group' in a classroom context? In many classrooms groups are simply batches of children around a set of furniture or a collection of children engaged on the same individual task.

When teachers are asked what sort of groupings they use, they tend to use terms that can be vague or convey different meanings to different people, such as 'ability group', 'mixed ability group' or 'friendship group'. However, these terms betray themselves if used without care.

Ability groups
An ability group is often a subtle form of inability group. The problem with abilities in classrooms is that they come in various guises: some children are able in skills but unable in concepts, others are able in concepts but not in expression, and so the task of putting children in ability groups is very difficult.

Mixed ability groups
Ability groups are more difficult to apply to mathematics where a child can be competent in numeracy but is struggling within areas of conceptual understanding. Hence teachers go for mixed ability groups, small groups comprising children with various skills and crafts, skills and abilities, skills and understanding. However, is constructing mixed ability groups any more efficient than simply randomly grouping children and hoping for the best?

Friendship groups
Some teachers use friendship groups, asking children who they would like to work with. Since, like adults, children have different friendships for different activities, they must be offered the opportunity to change groups at appropriate times. Indeed, many children are not aware of working in a group since they are allocated to a table collection early in the year and find they are still in the same 'group' in June.

These three types of group are all collections for some reason or other, but effective group work in the classroom can go beyond this.

Abilities levels are one crucial aspect, but there are others. Restricted resources are a major pressure on teachers: a limited area for reading, limited equipment for mathematics. If art equipment is limited, art activities can only be offered to a certain number of children at once. Children are put into groups to do individual clerical activities because everybody in that group is doing that at the time. These are organisational strategies for teachers rather than genuine group work.

What is genuine group work?

This takes place when children actively collaborate with each other to achieve a finished product. Group work has been discussed in primary schools since *The Plowden Report* (1967), but research continues to highlight the extreme rarity of collaboration in classrooms. Even though classrooms are arranged to encourage interaction between children, the level of expected interaction is often minimal. Genuine groups encourage children to work together, and there are significant reasons why this is worthwhile.

1 Working with others is an education in itself. Effective group work is one way of encouraging qualities such as collaboration and co-operation. Working together creates genuine learning opportunities.
2 By working together children are more likely to monitor their own efforts than to rely on the teacher. This is extremely important if children are to be encouraged to be independent and responsible for their own ideas and actions. When the teacher is present, even on the periphery, children are more likely to turn to them for approval. When there is no teacher available, children are more likely to predict, lay out the options and select one that makes sense, summarise and report back in much greater detail for themselves. They then have to stand by their decisions.
3 Working in a group is likely to encourage talk about the task in hand rather than social gossip. Most teachers articulate the view that talk matters in learning, indeed the National Curriculum and 5-14 Guidelines emphasise the importance of speaking and listening as a way of learning. If children are engaged in the same mathematical task, they are much more likely to stay on that task and to work towards solving it. The talk that emanates from the group is more likely to be talk which matters to their learning. Teachers will need to check individual children's learning but working in a proper group will keep children focused on the task.

If such group work is to take place in the classroom then careful thought must be given to the sorts of groups used. This means going beyond ability and friendship thinking into organisational thinking and trying to establish routines and patterns for organisation within the classroom.

What other sorts of groups are there?

Brainstorm groups

Brainstorm groups are a simple way of encouraging children to co-operate. A group of children are given a sheet of paper and a pen and one person writes down the ideas that the rest call out. Not only is this useful for speaking, listening and working as a group, but it is a practice that is encouraged when writing for different purposes; it also helps the assessment process by giving the teacher an insight into the sorts of thinking that children do. It is important to establish the ground rules. No child's effort is rejected; nobody's ideas are regarded as too silly. The brainstorm group is one way of encouraging children genuinely to work as a group and to come up with ideas or suggestions.

The snowball group

Snowball groups take the members of one brainstorm group and encourage them to swap with another group so they can add ideas and suggestions and build on what is already there. Snowball groups can build up from two to four to eight so that a collection of ideas, is built up within the class. For example, children can offer ideas for stories or suggest ideas for the meanings of Egyptian hieroglyphics. Different mathematical patterns might circulate or pieces of research about famous Victorians.

Work can take place over some time: one group starts off a process with ideas, a second group offers further solutions, a third group makes further suggestions, or perhaps criticisms, over a period of days or weeks. The important thing is that the children collaborate to build up a bigger picture.

The expert or specialist group

Some children can study a topic or technique in detail and as a group become experts upon it. They are then able to tell other children in the classroom what they have learnt. Beyond this they could become the class specialists within the routines of the classroom, for example four children can become the class specialists on how the library works. Small groups of children can become specialists on very small aspects of classroom work that concern skills as opposed to knowledge and understanding. Once those children are experts or specialists they can begin to transmit their learning to other groups.

Visiting other groups

When several groups are working at once to solve a problem in technology or science, one person from each group could visit the other groups to see what they are doing and report back to their own group. This is a quick way to spread ideas and it also helps to point out to children the importance of co-operating and sharing ideas rather than competing with each other.

Too often, in order to make groups work, teachers try to ensure an adult presence. This is a valuable source of learning for many children but it is not essential. Children can be encouraged to learn, given effective curriculum objectives, when there is no adult present as long as they are given the right physical conditions for their learning. The teacher's role is to make sure the conditions are right and the groups can work together.

Helping groups to work

As with all things, children need to learn how to work in a group. It is easy to say that it will not work because some children cannot cope. The teacher should take the initiative and help children to develop the skills necessary and give group work a chance for it to be successful.

Think about the best size for a working group
Two children will usually work together as long as they have enough ideas. Three is a good size for a group: enough ideas and time for everyone to speak and listen. Four is just about the top number; maybe too many ideas and only just enough time to contribute. If there are five in a group it is too big. Group members are too far apart physically and there is a battle for the floor when they want to speak. Five will usually split into two smaller groups. Six will also split. Problems arise when these bigger groups split and someone gets left out. In the classroom the spare ones can cause problems and allowances must be made for it.

What are the implications for seating arrangements in the primary classroom if two, three or four are optimal for a working group? So many teachers extol the virtues of talk and group work but still put children in table arrangements of six, eight, ten or more. These children have little chance of working together.

Sit children so that they can work together
If possible, children should try to sit in groups of no more than four. However, if space makes this impossible, the groups should be structured so the children can talk together in smaller numbers. Everyone in the group also needs to be able to see what they are supposed to be doing. It also helps if they can see it the right way up!

Teach appropriate skills
Children need to be taught to take turns, to listen, to record and to summarise. They cannot learn all these skills at once; they must work towards them gradually, for a short period of time, guided and conducted by the teacher.

Give children roles
Assign roles at the beginning. Ask one child to be timekeeper, another to record. Even numbering speakers early on can help to organise the conversation.

Give real collaborative tasks
Children are often seated in groups and given the same task but are not required to work in a group. They need one of everything per group and they need to produce their result as a group.

Talk to them as a group
It is so easy to look at a group of children and address individual children. After the teacher gives instructions it is for the group to sort out whether it understands and it is for them to define and solve any

problems. Equally, praise or moans need to be given to the group, not to individuals. They have to sort out the congratulations themselves.

Start small
The most important aspect of starting small is the size of the group. Start with pairs of children working together and build up from there. Short times, small tasks, clear outcomes, success, one other group as an audience - all these will help to get group work going.

Paired work

If the pairs are set short tasks, working together for a few minutes at a time, the children will become used to challenging, questioning and supporting each other. The skills they learn and develop can then be gradually transferred to other, more extended tasks.

Paired spelling challenges

- Give each pair one sheet of paper and two pens. Make them sit so that they can both see the paper from the same angle. One is the writer and the other is the helper.
- The teacher calls out a word and the writer has a go at writing it. The helper watches the word being written and then either agrees or works with the writer to alter, amend and adjust the spelling until the pair have an agreed spelling for the word. The paper becomes a working sheet for their efforts.
- The teacher can call out one word and after a while give another, and then another. The writer will have written a first response and the pair will talk about any of the words once there are a few written down.

There are several values in this paired approach:

1 Spelling is a visual skill. Some people spell using the 'learn it by letter - sound it out' approach but most people need to look at words to help them spell correctly. Good spellers know when a word does not 'look right' when they are writing. They know that there are options and often try several before picking the best looking one. If children are to be good, confident spellers they must be encouraged to look closely at words and discuss the way they are put together. They must be allowed to consider the possibilities, perhaps using a friend as a sounding board.

2 Children are frequently given words to learn for a spelling test. Problems can arise from the approaches children adopt to learn the words. Some children seem able just to glance at the words, remember them, have a quick revision glance on the fateful day, and all goes well. Other children attempt to memorise the words one by one, chanting the letters and repeating mistakes until they become natural. They could rehearse the words for weeks without getting anywhere. When the pairs look at the words during the week, children can have their attention drawn to the way words are spelled. They can return to the same words each day and remember with their friend which part of the word is the bit to watch for. They can see the patterns in a family of words because their friend seems to jot that bit down on autopilot. Children gain confidence by being offered chances to explore what they do and do not understand, rather than only being shown that they are not very good.

Options for the word lists include:

- **Words from yesterday**
  The same words repeated for several days running and returned to a couple of weeks later.
- **Words from this week's test**
  Some of the words that are on the list, some the same, some different each day.
- **Words from children's own writing**
  If commonly mis-spelt words are chosen, children's attention is drawn to the challenge of spelling words correctly.
- **Words offered by children**
  Asking the children to volunteer a word with which they have struggled in their writing 'today' encourages children to take risks in writing because it values the efforts of people who are trying new and difficult things. It is also good to ask children to offer words which they thought of using but decided not to because the spelling was complex! How good for the struggler to offer words that are then written by the whole class.

The spelling challenges need not last long. Five or ten minutes a day, including the answers, is plenty. The answers do not need to be recorded. It does not matter how many were right or wrong. What matters is that the children are looking at the words and discussing the patterns.

Calculation pairs
This is very similar to the paired spelling challenges but the focus is upon calculations. Children sit in pairs sharing a sheet of paper; one is the writer and one is the checker. A few minutes writing followed by discussion is all that is needed each day.

1 **Speed bonds**
The teacher calls out simple number problems using the four rules but moving from addition to multiplication and so on. The writer puts down the answers only, working at speed. The problems are not repeated and there is only a five-second gap between each. The checker watches the answers as they are written and, after five answers, tells the writer whether they are correct.

Usually, there is total silence and the checker tries to work out the answer before the writer puts pencil to paper. Most children will do this so that they have an answer in mind before one appears, so that they are not confused by the answer that is written. This activity, repeated two or three times with checkers and writers exchanging will, over time, encourage the children to work at speed in simple calculations.

A useful side-effect occurs when a struggler who is acting as a checker finds that they can beat the writer in calculation; they realise that when they do mathematics it is the clerical task of writing the answer that holds them up rather than the calculation itself. So many slow writers get frustrated by their inability to write the answers and by the view of other people that they must be slow learners.

2 'Do it and tell it maths'
A calculation is written on the paper - the typical 'four rules of number, double or triple digit' problem, perhaps with a bit of carrying. The writer does the calculation and 'talks it out'. The children talk about how it is done, which bits are difficult, where it is going wrong, and why it is not right; they talk out loud about the things that should be going on in their heads. The calculations do not have to be simple. They can involve algebra, equations, a series of problems using calculators, anything that gives the children the chance to explain their actions.

3 Check it back
The teacher gives a calculation which will result in the answer being part of another calculation. A previous subtraction will leave an answer which can be added to one of the original numbers to reveal the other. Children will do the additions and gradually realise that they could carry out this step earlier. One important aspect of mathematics is learning to self check; the teacher should be delighted when children announce that they know their calculation is correct because they have 'worked it backwards'.

Little pairs
Children do not have to be able to do complex writing tasks in order to work together. As long as the idea of one as the 'doer' and one as the checker is established, the use of paired working in short bursts is a valuable approach.

1 **Picking plastic**
Stack a big heap of coloured cubes in the middle of the table. The children sit in pairs, one to pick, one to check. The teacher calls out the pieces to be picked. The picker picks, the checker checks and the pair adjust if necessary; within twenty seconds the cubes are back in the heap ready for the next go.

Instructions can be:
three reds;
three of the same colour;
two of one colour, two of another;
two blues, two yellows, two pinks, two whites;
one red, one blue, one red in between two yellows
and so on, depending upon the complexity of mathematics, colours or language you want to exploit. There could be a week of varying the numbers while keeping other aspects constant, or a week where the emphasis is upon the colours.

2 **Mixing money**
Coins, plastic or real, are put in a heap on the table, with pairs of children sitting around. As with the plastic it is picked, checked and put back at speed.

3 **Early writers**
As children start to write they need plenty of practice in short, sharp bursts; one way forward is to use checking partners. As before, give one piece of paper to two children, one to write, one to check and both to talk.

Instructions can be:
two triangles;
a different-sized triangle;
a different-shaped triangle;
a capital 'r';
an arrow pointing downwards;
a longer arrow pointing upwards;
a rectangle;
a big circle;
a circle inside the circle ....

All these very short tasks help children to follow instructions, make them listen to language, demand a response and gain instant feedback, at speed.

Story chats
Imagine the start of the story, *'In this story there are four cats'*. The teacher starts to turn the page but is interrupted by offerings from the class of listeners on the floor.

'My gran has a cat and it brings back mice and puts them under

the table.'
'That's very interesting. We'll have to see if that happens in this story.'
'There was a cat down our street and it got run over by a motor bike and there was all blood and ...'
'That doesn't sound very nice.'
'Our cat had kittens and my dad got a bucket of ...'
'Well, we aren't talking about your cats, are we? We are talking about the four cats in the book. They are really interesting.'

But just as the teacher takes breath to start, a little voice at the front murmurs, 'I don't like cats anyway'.

'You'll like these cats.'
'I've read it and I didn't like it.'

A familiar experience? You want the children to be involved, but they do not yet understand that this is not the time for involvement? They are doing what adults do. They are getting ready to receive the story. They are acting like real readers and getting ready to respond, in fact they have started to respond. Good readers do the same thing but they have learned to think rather than say it.

One of the greatest causes of concern for teachers in children's behaviour is 'talking out of turn'. One of the reasons children talk out of turn is that they never get a turn. So how about trying again?

'This story is called 'The four cats'. It is by the same author as yesterday's story. In your twos, talk for two minutes about the story.'

Once the children get the idea they will talk in the way adults do when discussing a book or a film. Have they read it before? Did they enjoy it? What do they think it is about? Have they ever had a cat? At the end of two minutes they will have said the things that needed saying to someone.

After the story, what usually happens? The teacher says something like:

'Did you enjoy that story?' or
'You enjoyed that, didn't you?' or
'That was a good story, wasn't it?'

It takes a brave or socially unaware child to say, 'Actually, it was a bit boring and the storyline was contrived' not understanding that it was not a real question.

The teacher would then ask the important questions about the book: The questions might tell the children what they should have been thinking about and devalue the things that they thought were important or wondered about. Your questions matter ... but so do theirs.

How about allowing two minutes when children can talk to their friends before the start of general discussion? They might talk about:

- the important events
- the bits they really liked
- the bits they did not understand
- the fact that they found the story boring
- what was the point of the story?

Again they are acting like real readers, but in their two minutes they are more likely to talk about what matters to them rather than answer a maximum of one class question from the teacher.

Talking about books and stories can be extended to talk about information texts, poems, charts, diagrams, maps, prayers and hymns. Anything that teachers want children to engage with; they will talk about what matters to them and be all the more ready to listen to the teacher. Story chats work with children of any age.

Hunting partners

For young readers it is a good idea to go on a hunt through some well loved or slightly less familiar books. They can hunt for lots of things.

1 **Question mark hunting**

In twos, children search a book for a question mark. When one is found they have to read the part leading up to the question mark so that they get the flow of the story and the right intonation. They practise ready to read out to others if selected.

There are lots of benefits:

- The children see question marks!
- They read aloud but not too much.
- They read what they have practised so they are secure and they read with a friend for confidence.
- The level of intonation and the degree of exaggeration will grow with confidence.
- Confidence will grow by enjoying exploring the books for a little while but often.

The same 'hunt' can be done with exclamation marks.

2 **Speech mark spotting**

Same again, but this time the children need to use voices and sometimes more than two people are needed.

3 **Dictionary darting**

In twos, the teacher suggests the word and the children try to find the meaning. This is a paired activity that can be broken down into a more directed activity with the teacher conducting the finder and the checker. Suppose the word to be found is 'replenished'; the finders could indicate where they think the section is. The checker opens the dictionary. The teacher asks whether it is forwards or backwards from there; the finder indicates, the checker opens, and so on. The 'r' section is reached, then 're', then 'repl'. After that, of course, comes the point of looking it up: the meaning. They need to remember that because next week there could be a paired challenge, where children try to write down meanings from memory, in pairs of course.

4 Atlas antics

One atlas between two, the teacher names a city and the two children have to find it. Using the index may be easier but they may need guidance as in the dictionary example.

Word explorers

The basic pattern is the same but the children work in twos to find examples, either at speed to share with the rest of the class or over time as they see things in their general routine.

1 Find the syllables

The children write the word 'at'. How many words can they write that begin with the sound 'at'? The children work at this for about five minutes. As children call out their answers, note how many syllables each word uses. For children to be good spellers they need to listen to syllables rather than try to spot each letter. An activity like this stresses the syllables, especially if the teacher does not talk about the length of a word in letters. If the correct spellings are listened to, commented upon in terms of meaning or the number of syllables, but not spelt out, the offerings will keep coming. Children will offer long words they have written, even though they are not spelled correctly. So many children do not use long words in writing because there is a greater chance of spelling it incorrectly. This activity, done regularly, will give children confidence to use long words. It is also worth realising that if they can read them out they do not need to follow the teacher around the class asking for spellings at the early stage of a piece of writing. They can get the word onto the paper themselves by writing what it sounds like. The spelling can be worked on later.

2 Hide the sound

The children make a list of words which contain 'at' but where those two letters do not say 'at'. The sound is something else in many words. The children can work on this in pairs for ten minutes or so and a composite list can be made on the board.

The first offering might be 'station' and others in that list might be 'illustration', 'nation', and 'creation'. The next offering could be 'seat', to which could be added 'neat', 'wheat', and 'pleat'; but not 'breath', because that would go in another list. And so it goes on. Both during this session and later children can add to the list and find different variations on the sound of that little syllable.

Word explorers shows children how complicated sounds and spelling are. It helps them to become fascinated by the language and to look for patterns which help them make sense of it.

Avoiding problems with paired work

There are so many advantages with paired work but there are possible problems.

1 Some teachers worry that the children will copy each other. That is the idea. For a short period each day the children have a chance to ask someone how to proceed, to get ideas. Think about the way adults learn things; by asking when you get the chance, by watching someone else, by puzzling it out together, even by helping someone else. Working together is not the entire answer. The teacher still needs to check each child understands.

2 It worries some people that children see wrong answers. It need not be a problem. Children who can do something confidently delight in being able to identify, quietly, where someone else has gone wrong. The notion of picking the best guess from lots of possibilities is an important one in learning, and children must be given a chance to do this. Children are more confident learners when they can see the mass of possible mistakes to avoid, especially the tricky and cunning ones.

3 A major concern is that some children are lazy and let others do all the work. This is a danger but it is probably as big a problem when children are in a whole class situation. Some children are prone to cruising, and being in a pair will not make it worse. It might make it better. The teacher has to avoid being the arbitrator who offers to sort out disagreements. If the work is quick enough there is no time anyway!

4 A useful technique is to allow children to select their partners for the first few sessions. After, say, three goes the partners have to change. The original partnerships cannot reform until each child has worked with five more partners. The children do not mind who they work with once they have got going. Also the striders and the strugglers do not mind working together, in fact they often head straight for each other because each partner enjoys the five-minute activity. Children may get on better together in the classroom if they are allowed to mix occasionally for work.

Using groups to ...

Using groups does not have to be difficult or complicated. One way of looking at it is to think of situations in the classroom when other children can be used as a resource:
Consider what has been said - children can think about the topic together and test each others' ideas
Find out what they already know - gives children the chance to ask questions of each other
Admit misunderstandings - finds out what the children do not understand before the work comes in
Get ideas - ideas seem easier when the task is shared
Add to ideas - each group passes their ideas to another group, which adds to and amends them; by the time the ideas return there are plenty to choose from
Identify important ideas, issues, skills - makes children prioritise and compare viewpoints and gives feedback to the teacher.

Many teachers worry about trying to provide real group situations in classrooms. They find themselves struggling to develop suitable activities. The staff of one primary school decided to make a concerted effort to provide such situations in classrooms and two teachers agreed to try. They did different things but went through a series of planning stages in order to help them develop confidence. The teachers each chose a different starting point but took the big step of having a go *(see pages 43-44)*.

Developing productive talk in real group situations

Age range	Year 2
Task	To plan an infant Friday assembly.
Classroom layout	Tables already arranged in groups of two.

Starting point

All children sitting on the 'learning carpet!' Initial whole class discussion, teacher led. 'We're doing the assembly tomorrow.'

Series of questions

What happens in a Friday assembly?
How will we know who has a birthday?
What songs will we sing?
How will the classes be arranged, i.e. seating?
Will we make a class contribution?
How long will it last?
How will the classes come in and go out?
Who will introduce the assembly?

Into groups

This was the fourth time that the children had participated in such an activity so all I needed to say was "get yourselves into groups of three".

They were given a five minute time limit for initial discussion. Large sheets of paper and coloured pens were then handed out. Ten minutes for brainstorming session. Just jottings, no need to worry about correct spelling. At the end of time we passed the papers around and they read each others' ideas. Five more minutes to add anything else. Back to whole class discussion. Programme drawn up: Children to interview Mrs Spence about music. Mrs Ashford and Mrs Town to be asked how they knew who had a birthday. Wanted to re-arrange the seating for the assembly, great frustration at not being able to see. Classes to sit in a semi-circle, so only three rows deep instead of nine.

What did the children get out of it?

- When we began the majority of the class hadn't got a clue about what went on during assembly. They obviously went in, switched off or messed about! They really had to focus their thoughts on the problem, it was real, it was going to happen tomorrow. They talked, expressed opinions, argued points, persuaded, wrote, helping each other to spell the words in an unthreatening situation.
- The discussion about timing involved a lot of maths. How long is an assembly anyway? As long as playtime? As long as a PE lesson?
- They had to go and interview members of staff and come back with satisfactory answers.
- Mrs Cousins was interviewed to negotiate some Hall time.
- They realised that they had been working very hard.
- Tremendous sense of achievement on Friday morning. Everyone pulled their weight, it was their project, they basked in their success.

My reactions

Initially it was very noisy! What if visitors are being shown around the school! Am I disturbing the class next door? But after the initial surge of enthusiastic volume it moderated. The most difficult thing was holding back. Let the children do the talking, but tune in to what is being said.

You must sum up. Tell the children how hard they have been working. Only then will they view the activity as work. Try to repeat the activity on a regular basis. You will find that after a while the nature of talk in the classroom changes from gossip to talk about the work in hand. Once you jump in and try you will find it both easy and very rewarding.

Developing productive talk in real group situations

Age range Year 5
Classroom layout No change needed as session divided into 2, half the class at art.

Starting points

Part of the cross curricular topic work on China. Class has been discussing the importance of tea production. Sets of ten postcards detailing the process of tea production in China from planting to sale were shown to the large group. The children were asked to put the cards in order.

Into groups

The children were split into small groups of three. This was the first time that such an activity had been tried so the groups were chosen by the teacher. Strong personalities shared out, quieter members of the class scattered among the groups. After ten minutes or so of intense talk, the groups were re-formed. Views were shared, opinions voiced, then regrouping again. Back to large group to decide on an order that would be acceptable to everyone.

Length of session About 45 minutes.

What did the children get out of it?

- They learnt far more about tea production than they ever would have done from listening to a 'lecture', or looking in a book.
- Their observational skills were used to the full.
- They made predictions, formed hypotheses.
- They had to use previous knowledge to help them order the cards.
- They had to produce reasoned arguments to convince their peers.
- They had to co-operate.
- They had to think quickly to reach a conclusion within a time limit.

Teacher's reactions

Found it very exciting way of working. Not nearly as noisy as she had imagined (but only half a class!). Found it extremely difficult to stand back and not get involved in the discussions.

Was able to observe the way the children handled the situation. Weaker children shone through. Dominant children had to learn to co-operate. If they didn't they missed out.

Will do it again.

7 *Reducing interruptions*

Every teacher knows the problem of interruptions, and most would love to know a solution. It would be too simplistic to advise on how to deal with children who interrupt; as with any other challenge in the classroom, a procedure is needed to try to put it right. So in the case of interruptions the points are:

- Why do children interrupt?
- Strategies to reduce interruptions
- Checking and reinforcing.

Why do children interrupt?

Most classroom teachers could give any number of reasons why children interrupt. However, teachers rarely talk about two reasons, which may underlie many children's visits to a teacher who is trying to do something else:

'It's what grown-ups do'
Perhaps children interrupt because they see grown-ups interrupting teachers. In many schools teachers working in their classrooms are constantly interrupted by other adults. The children with the teacher can be in the midst of a mystic experience sharing a poem when, two lines from the end, there is a feeble tap at the door. After several calls to come in, a child enters, in a hesitant dithering way, usually with a friend. They bring an important message from an adult: news of measles injections or cycling proficiency, and within an instant the mystic experience of the poem is lost, gone for ever, and the interruption assumes importance. There are vital messages here for whole school approaches and whole school decision making.

Next time you are going to send a message around school, it is worth asking yourself whether the message is important enough to interrupt the learning of every single pupil or whether it could wait for a staff meeting.

'It's what teachers want'
Teachers talk about children being independent; schools have aims about children taking decisions and being responsible for themselves; and yet in many classrooms children are given the impression that teachers want them to interrupt.

> *'If you don't know what to do just come and ask.'*
> *'If you're stuck then I'll come and try to help you.'*
> *'If it doesn't work let me know.'*

Do the resulting conversations encourage effective learning? Are they centred around the curriculum? Or are they a running commentary on a classroom where children think that to be good means to visit the teacher?

Strategies to reduce interruptions

Maybe the staff should consider strategies that will be applied across the whole school in an effort to encourage children to think carefully about the issue.

1 **Setting expectations**

Has the teacher really ever told the children that being a good pupil in the classroom means trying not to interrupt the teacher and attempting to sort the problem out for themselves? Children usually find out that interruptions are not wanted when the teacher finally erupts, however nicely, and explains that she has had enough for today and they must all please go back and get on. This is different from calmly pointing out to children, regularly and before there is a problem, that being a good pupil in the classroom means sorting yourself out and trying not to interrupt the teacher. For many children the only way to get attention and to be complimented is to get into a queue and wait to meet the teacher. Children need to be recognised for trying to sort things out for themselves.

How about making a list with the children of all the things they can do for themselves, that they are able to organise and manage without interrupting the teacher?

2 **Resourcing**

Most classroom teachers understand the need to make resources accessible and available to children. Teachers go to great lengths to label and store resources so that children can find them for themselves. They colour code, number, label, picture label or even silhouette where things should go in the classroom so that children can manage and organise their own resources. However, the area that might save interruptions is the one that is often neglected.

How about practising putting resources away? During lunchtime, take simple resources from around the classroom and put one resource between each pair of children. As the children enter the classroom they need to sit down and discuss where their resource is kept. Do they know *precisely* where that resource goes in the classroom? They may have a book, but the book corner is not the answer. Do they know which shelf in the book corner? It may be colour coded or number referenced in a catalogue system for information books, it may be an outsized book which goes on a special shelf. If they have a computer disk, to suggest 'near the computer' is not precise enough. Better to say, 'in a wallet in a specific place in the IT area'.

If the children know where their object goes, fine. If not, they can swap and different partners can have a go. When a pair is confident, they can replace the resource exactly where it belongs. If they do not know then the teacher can explain, and explain the reasons and give the children the opportunity to put it away. That resource then becomes one that regularly appears after lunch for the pairs to discuss over the next month or so.

This activity does not need to be done every day, but ten minutes spent regularly will mean that children will become at ease with the resources in the classroom and with putting them away. If they can put them away in exactly the right places, they do not have to follow the teacher around to ask where they can find equipment.

3 Two answers

This is a good strategy but it takes a while to get going. The basic premise is that instead of children queuing up, reaching the front of the queue and saying things like 'I forgot why I came' they have to come to the teacher with a question.

In one school this was tried because the children were interrupting incessantly and the teachers decided that drastic action was needed. The teachers said to the children, *'We like talking to you, but you do come to see us rather too much. So we are going to say that you can still come and see us, but when you come you must have a question. If you haven't got a question you will be told to go away. But not only must you have a question, you must also have two possible answers and be able to say which is the better answer.'*

The strategy does not work for a long time because when the children eventually get to speak to the teacher they still say, 'I don't know what my question is'. At this point they must be given no reward but told to go and sit down. Later they remember the question but they have not thought of two possible answers. Eventually the children get used to the idea and the pattern continues; whatever the child says is the better answer is what they do.

In the school that tried this idea, it worked after about three weeks with Year 6. As Year 6 got the idea it was possible to see the pattern running down right through to the reception class. After about eight weeks most of the school were able to go through the process. Once it is working it starts to have an impact. After a while the children get fed up with queuing and thinking of questions and answers and they solve their own problems. Once they have sorted themselves out the number of interruptions does not just drop, it plummets.

In practice it was found that the interruptions diminished, and also a better level of conversation was possible. Because there were fewer interruptions the teachers could talk in depth with the children. Now the conversation went something like, 'My question is, how do I colour this piece of painting. The best two answers are "this reddish brown colour that I've mixed here" and "this yellowish brown colour that I've mixed here on my palette". I think the better answer is this reddish brown'. The teacher can then follow this up and say, *'Yes that's probably the best colour; how are you actually going to apply it? Are you going to hatch it, or spot it, or are you going to water colour it on the page?'* What develops is a quality conversation about art.

It takes time and hard work to get going, but when it works it is worthwhile, especially if it is introduced right through the school.

4 A good instruction pattern

To watch good instructors is to appreciate their skill. They use techniques that are only apparent when they are pointed out. Good instructors:

- use the same starts for sentences several times
- offer headlines before they move forward to the main body of their instructions, *'I am going to tell you three things, number one, number two and number three.'*
- use eye contact, posture and gesture to hold the attention of their audience
- spread their arms in front of them when they offer a wide explanation
- make a splitting action with their hand when they split things into sections.

The skill of instruction is something to be studied and thought through.

Whatever the instruction or the method used, consider offering instruction, summarising, and then asking the children whether there is anybody who does not understand. If nobody says they do not understand it can be assumed that everyone does. Once the task has started, the first person to interrupt is politely but firmly told that they had their chance to say they did not understand. The chance has gone.

5 'When I say'

So often when instructions are given to children, they act at the first opportunity. They are not listening to the rest of the instructions and the teacher is besieged with questions about what they have to do next.

To avoid this problem try saying, *'When I say, I want you to get out your ruler, your maths book, your pencil and a piece of paper'.* Then say, *'Right, I'm saying it now'*. It sounds simple, but actually children need to be held back until the moment comes to go, and when they all understand what they have got to do, then to be told, 'Off we go'.

6 Guess the interruption

This is a strategy which can have enormous impact providing it is handled in the right way. Having given good instructions, got the children ready and made sure that everybody understands what they have to do, the children are invited to spend a couple of minutes guessing what interruptions might occur.

By playing Guess the Interruption the children who are most likely to interrupt are put on the spot by their own classmates. Moreover, it becomes apparent to them that everybody in the room understands what they interrupt for, why they do it and how much they interrupt. Care needs to be taken that children are not humiliated but this strategy can open up some problems.

7 Time trials

Explain to the children everything that needs to be done. Make sure they all understand, let them guess the interruptions, and then challenge them to see if they can work for ten minutes without anybody asking anything.

The children start and the teacher does not get involved with any group but simply watches the classroom. While it is running well, let it run, but as soon as it starts to go, stop the children and explain, *Well done, you've worked for exactly ten minutes without any interruption'*, regardless of how long the time has been. Tell them that they succeeded in the challenge and managed ten minutes with no interruptions. If it was eight minutes what does it matter? If children think that they can last for ten minutes with no interruptions maybe they will expect to be able to do so next time.

When the children can last for ten minutes, try moving it up to twelve, fifteen, twenty, twenty-five, all the time trying to explain to them what being good in the classroom means in terms of interrupting teachers.

The strategies are there to try. They may work for you, but you need to check and constantly reinforce to children the simple message that interruption is not good behaviour.

Checking and reinforcing

Catching good attempts

One of the best ways to encourage desirable behaviour is to catch children doing things right. If the right behaviour is continually emphasised instead of only finding fault, children are more likely to know what is good. Most children wish to please their teacher by doing what they think is good, so catching good attempts is an admirable practice.

The problem with catching good attempts in this context is that to praise children because they have not interrupted, the teacher will probably have to interrupt their work, which is self-defeating. Teachers must think of ways to let children know that their efforts to avoid interrupting have been noticed. At the end of a session, for example, stop the class and announce that, *'Peter has been very good because when he got stuck with his work, he tried different ways to sort it out for himself'*. Or *'Amritt was really good; she was superb in the session because when she couldn't spell some of the words she was writing she practised for herself on a piece of paper and picked the best option'*. Or *'John behaved excellently because, when he needed the equipment for his maths problem, he went and got it for himself, organised it and put it back when he had finished with it'*.

By noting down occasions during the session when children organise themselves rather than interrupt, good attempts can be recognised rather than problems.

Thinking back

At the end of the session a few minutes can be put aside to encourage children to think back over their actions in the last hour. Can children identify times when they interrupted and why? A list or a graph could be kept to indicate trends and patterns.

Can children identify occasions when they might have interrupted but found a way not to do so? Over time a list of alternatives to interruptions could be built up, and this could form the basis for future discussions and graphs.

Setting expectations

By trying these strategies and constantly reinforcing the idea that being a good pupil in the classroom entails not interrupting the teacher, interruptions can be reduced. If these strategies make even a few children think again about whether it is appropriate to interrupt the teacher, then it will encourage the qualities that most teachers identify as being significant attributes for learning. Independence, confidence, responsibility, making decisions and risk taking are qualities that are not gained in a queue, they are gained by children thinking for themselves.

8 *Using other adults in the classroom*

Many primary classrooms have adults other than the teacher working in them. This might be classroom assistants, Section 11 teachers, SEN support, parents, student teachers or work experience pupils from secondary schools. Other adults offer possibilities for widening curriculum opportunities. However, they require organisation and there are issues to consider if the children are to gain maximum benefit.

Give attention to all activities
It is very tempting to use the extra adult to cover the basics and asking them only to listen to readers. This may give children the idea that this basic activity is more important than the other things they do. There are other dangers. If the parent does sewing or art with the children while the teacher catches up on the 'basics', the children can easily think that the art or the play area is not important because the 'basic' is what the teacher does and the extra help does the frills. It is essential to communicate to children that all learning in the classroom is important, well planned and purposeful, and to plan the way in which adults will help support or leave children to make their own decisions.

Make one available, the other busy
If there is more than one adult in the classroom, one adult could be busy with a group or an individual on one task, and therefore not available at all. The group is getting good attention and uninterrupted time, and the other adult is available to help. The available adult should be free to be called upon, and should not go around intervening or making suggestions.

Use the adult in different ways

- **The participant**

  At times the extra adult can be a participant within the children's activity, to demonstrate that the outcome is not predetermined by adults but is actually a result of the thinking and the work that takes place. Any adult who genuinely joins in when the children are trying to write a story, will be honestly able to say how difficult the task of writing a story is, not just for children but for anybody, and will give the teacher a clear idea of what the children are asked to do. The children will also gain a clearer idea of the difficulty of some of the things they do in the classroom.

- **The observer**

The job of the teacher can be easier if others observe how children cope with particular tasks. The observer who can devote real time to watching will pick up where a child is managing easily and where they are frustrated or failing in learning. It might be a planned piece of assessment but equally it could be a view of how an infant is getting on socially in the domestic play area.

- **The scribe**

Using the adult to scribe for a child or group of children takes away one big blockage for children's ideas, the clerical task. Children will be pleased to have ideas if someone else will write them down. The adult doing the writing is a real model for children. Writing quickly, struggling with difficult words, making mistakes and correcting them, having a go, are all features of a good writer that can be demonstrated by the scribe.

- **The gofer**

The other adult is most commonly used as a gofer, someone who does the dogsbody jobs, and often enjoys doing them. However, before long the children see this other adult as someone who will do anything, go for anything, which means they do not have to think for themselves.

- **The checker**

The adult can be the one who checks, the final arbiter. They could check that the child or group can mix paint, really do the mathematics problem or find a word in the dictionary. For the teacher it is the perfect test, for children it is a chance to show someone else what they can do.

- **The audience**

Another adult becomes a wonderful audience. An adult who has not been there all the time is the one to listen to a story written by children. The child is offering their efforts to someone who was not involved in the writing and who comes to it fresh. The adult can ask genuine questions, questions to which they do not know the answer, and children can engage in real conversations about their work.

- **The reviewer**

Using the other adult to look back on the child's work will give the teacher insights into the success of the learning experience. The teacher can devise a method of review, perhaps with a form to complete, or can simply ask the other adult to spend some time with a child or a group to find out what they thought of the work they have done. The adult could consider whether the child has understood the task, whether there were any big problems, what the child thinks has been learned and what the child thinks the point of the work was.

The use of other adults in the classroom raises so many questions that it might be worth asking a few of yourself. There are four sets of questions about classroom assistants on pages 54-55. You could give them to the assistants and ask them to identify the important ones. Work through the questions and pull out those that really matter. Then try to do something about the answers. Classroom assistants have so much to offer and have lots of ideas and enthusiasm.

Questions about Classroom Assistants

Effective use of classroom assistant time across the school

* Is what they are doing beneficial to children?
* How much time do they waste and whose fault is it?
* Are they given a programme to follow?
* Do you use their skills, strengths?
* Should everyone be given the same amount of time?
* What principles do you use to divide ancillary time between year groups/key stages?
* Have you asked your ancillaries what particular skills they have in order to make use of them?
* Do your ancillaries have preferences with year groups?
* Would it be better to allocate one ancillary to one teacher/year group than to spread five ancillaries across KS1 classes?
* Should all teachers have equal time?
* Is the allocation of classroom assistant time appropriate to the teacher e.g. are you out of class when you have an assistant?
* Is there a system for assistants to know what to do when one task is finished - avoiding interruptions?

The role of the classroom assistant

* Do you know the particular talents of each assistant?
* To what extent should they be involved in routine tasks, e.g. backing work, mixing paints!
* To what extent should they be involved in children's learning?
* Is the assistant present when children are given instructions?
* Are the assistant's skills put to best use?
* Do the children value the assistant?
* How do you feel you could improve their use?
* Should they have a job description?
* What status does the CA have?
* What is too much to ask, e.g. School policy on Health and Safety?
* What is the most important way in which a CA can support you in school?

Liaison and communication between the classroom assistant and teacher

* Is there any planning time?
* Have the classroom assistants been given the chance to voice their needs or concerns?
* Should classroom assistants be invited to staff meetings?
* What system do you use to communicate daily with your ancillary?
* Do you share break times with your ancillary?
* Is the CA included in dissemination of general information (school events etc)?
* Do you invite options?
* Is there an induction policy?

The responsibility of the teacher in mentoring the classroom assistant

* Is the teacher confident enough?
* Is there any induction process?
* Is there any time on on-going training?
* Is there time for evaluation/praise/criticism?
* Is there time for review (e.g. half-termly)?
* Do they have/do you have time to review the work the CA has done with children?
* What opportunities do you offer for your CA to ask questions and learn from you?
* Is there a need for INSET for ancillaries?
* Do you find it difficult to control/intervene in ancillary activities with children?
* Is there a need for one person to be the CA co-ordinator so they have someone to go to and the staff have a focal point?
* Should CAs be involved in INSET?
* How are ancillaries trained?
* What INSET is provided?
* If you expect an ancillary to do a job, how do you ensure that they are confident with skills/knowledge necessary?
* Are precise instructions given?
* Are classroom systems explained?

9 *Achieving good behaviour*

Off-task issues

Think of all the things that children do that take them off-task, not awful behaviour that is premeditated to cause offence to other children or the teacher, just minor distractions. If one child did one of these things it would not be a big problem; the cumulative effect of many children doing them together causes many problems.

Control devices

Primary teachers think of ways of controlling children to avoid the off-task distractions. Some of them are successful, some of them work for a little while and then lose their novelty. Others create more problems than they solve.

Top trouble-shooters
Here are some typical control systems and their side-effects:

- **'You can't go out until you've done it'**
  On a cold day, how does a child avoid their ten-minute stamp around outside at playtime? Answer - make sure they do not finish their work so that they can stay in!
- **'If you're naughty you'll have detention'**
  The silly thing about detention systems is that somebody has to supervise. After a while, the one who is suffering most is the teacher, who finds herself in detention day after day while the children seem to negotiate a rota to keep her there.
- **'You can't do your art until you've done your maths'**
  Play and work are balanced yet the children are given the idea that some aspects of the curriculum are more important than others. The side-effect is that some things appear to be valued and some things not, and if this is put alongside 'you can't go out until you've done it', problems increase instead of diminish.
- **'No swimming if you don't do your work'**
  This might work for most children, but what about the child who hates swimming, or the child who is reaching adolescence a little earlier than everybody else, or the very young child who is too shy to undress? The obvious way out of the embarrassment is to get banned from swimming by not doing work, playing up, or being really naughty.
- **Red marks and black marks**
  Marks for good behaviour, marks for bad behaviour: the immediate side-effect is that a race can develop, a race for red marks for those who can get red marks, and then, as it becomes clear that not everyone is really in the red mark race, a race for black marks develops. Anyone can get black marks just by doing naughty things, and naughty things are much easier to do than good things.

  Some schools modify these systems so that children cannot get more than five black marks, but again there are side-effects. A newly qualified teacher in such a school explains:

  'I thought the system was ridiculous; there was a great race at the beginning of term to get as many black marks as they could. The children strove to get black marks and I was giving them out as though there was no tomorrow. Before long everybody had four

black marks but I knew that when the fifth black mark was awarded they were thrown out of the house. I asked the head where they went when they were thrown out of the house. The head said that nobody was ever that bad and never in the history of the school had anybody ever reached five black marks. That was it, they'd got me over a barrel. They could do virtually what they liked now because so many had four that nobody could get the last, final black mark.'

- **Star charts**
  Since teachers generally reward academic work more than they reward social behaviour, star-gathering success is more open to children who can achieve well within the curriculum. These children quickly gain a mass of stars and move out so far in front of the class that they can rest on their laurels, enjoy themselves, misbehave even, for to lose a few stars is no great problem. Then, if some others start to challenge for leadership, they just submit some excellent academic work and move further away.
- **Nothing but rewards**
  Stars, badges and stickers, all those things that teachers give to encourage children to behave. Some teachers hold this as an answer: give only positive rewards and children will work to amass a collection. Nevertheless, there are still side-effects: before long children start to enquire in all sorts of subtle ways just what this piece of work is worth, and whether it should be more valuable than a previous piece of work. Sometimes, by the time a child starts on an activity, the teacher seems to have gone through a union negotiation!
- **The big gun**
  This strategy involves sending for somebody else. The head teacher is asked to come, and fires off a volley at naughty children. Alternatively the children can be sent to the head teacher. This immediately calms the children, but when the 'big gun' is not available the teacher's armoury is reduced. Furthermore, for every big gun there are lots of small guns around the school; every time the big gun is used the effectiveness of the small guns is reduced: the other teachers lose status in the children's eyes. Consequently, other adults in the school community lose their status too, so the classroom assistant, the student teachers who are on placement, the lunch time supervisors, all become less effective.

All of these trouble-shooters, or variations, are used in primary schools. It is questionable whether any of them are effective, for they seem to cause as many problems as they solve.

Within the classroom most teachers use small control devices to encourage children to behave well. While some of these have value, their side-effects often become more important than the control itself.

- **Hot seating**
  So that children do not call out and waste time, they are only allowed to speak if they are in the hot seat.
- **Circle time**
  A variation of the hot seat; children are given the opportunity to speak within the circle of other children when they are either holding the doll or the teddy bear, and everybody else is expected to listen.
- **Clicking, hand waving, clapping and fingers on lips**
  When the teacher wants attention they start up a system of movement which children join in with as they see it happening. This device attempts to control children physically by asking them to mimic the leader. Most teachers rely on it for no more than three weeks, after which they realise how ridiculous they look.
- **Whole class punishment**
  It still happens. Children are punished as a class for the transgressions of one or two children. Nothing is more likely to breed resentment, and resentment has endless side-effects.
- **Solitary confinement seating**
  A desk or chair is placed within the reach of the teacher's desk or chair so that a child who has transgressed is made to work alone. This works for some, but many children enjoy working alone since they get individual work. Within the peer group the child may boast that they have been on the solitary confinement seat more times than anyone else.
- **Sign up**
  Children are encouraged to sign up if they can do things for themselves. They sign up that they can use the library, the mathematics equipment, the computer. They sign up that they will be able to do their work unaided and without inhibiting anyone else. This is an attractive system because it gives the child the chance to exercise responsibility. The side-effects are seen when children sign up for things they are unable to do and create problems because of it.

Trouble-shooting systems, control devices and reward and punishment systems all deal with the consequences of behaviour. Classroom organisation should however seek to develop appropriate learning behaviour; the best way to develop that is through planning ahead. Typically, schools and teachers tend to look at pupil behaviour as a consequence. The eight steps to success described in Chapter 4 will help to avoid some of the discipline problems in schools. Trying the techniques described in Chapters 5 and 6 will help to avoid some of the difficulties in the classroom. Some children will always be naughty. The teacher should aim to deal with individual naughtiness rather than to develop watertight systems for every child in the classroom. Ways of achieving a positive working atmosphere are needed.

Reducing disruption - ways to get a positive working atmosphere

1 Let children know they can achieve

It is very easy to give children the idea that they will not be able to manage things and are expected to fail. This can be done in the way explanations are given, how they are helped, how they are pushed on. There is a thin line between wet nursing children across learning steps and throwing them in at the deep end; confidence for children, as for adults, is a very fragile thing. On the other hand, it is easy to trivialise work and give children the idea that anybody can do anything. The need to move children on is at the heart of teaching, children must be constantly challenged.

This places the focus upon the role of the teacher within the classroom. Teachers must constantly suggest to children that they can achieve, and that they can achieve more if they will accept a challenge, which has been set to try to move their learning on. Children need to be involved in the teacher's thinking and in their own learning.

2 Encourage learning risks

Those who learn most are the ones that are prepared to have a go. Teachers must have a clear understanding of what represents a mistake in the classroom. A mistake is a chance to learn. Used well, it can show how children's learning is proceeding and give the chance to move them on. However, if mistakes are confused with error and error confused with 'it doesn't matter', before long it is not learning risks that are encouraged, but classrooms where anything goes. Soon children recognise that they are not expected to achieve and the positive working atmosphere disappears.

3 Recognise children who are 'getting the idea'; show examples, broadcast success

Develop a success culture in the classroom because that encourages learning risks and lets children know that they are expected to achieve. Read out a good sentence at the start of a piece of writing. Talk about what children do well. Draw attention to it in a spirit of celebration. Moving children on provides a real opportunity to develop a working atmosphere.

4 Ensure appropriate resources are available

A positive working atmosphere is one where children do not spend time looking for materials. The frustration of this experience leads children away from the task in hand, which become counterproductive.

5 Do not publicise those who cannot do
This makes children cautious about taking learning risks because they become afraid of failure.

6 Have a go
Try joining in and writing a story and grappling with a few ideas, even getting an idea. It will demonstrate to children that the work you are asking them to do is very adult. Having a go yourself is a powerful way to develop a positive working atmosphere because it says to children that everyone is involved in a learning community and has got things to learn. At some times the teacher is the expert, leading children through stages and systems that she already understands, but at other times individual children can be the experts, leading all the learners through the stages that they understand.

7 Avoid broadcasting complaints
In some classrooms, a lot of time is spent broadcasting complaints about the noise level rather than praising behaviour. Much better broadcasts are those that say, *'It's good to see some people working really well', 'I've just seen a super start to a story'*. To convince children that things can be achieved and are working well, they have to be told. What the teacher announces has an impact on the classroom.

8 Public praise, private censure
Too often moans are made in public and children praised in private. This should be turned on its head: endeavour to praise publicly, not in an ingratiating or an embarrassing way, but tell children what is being achieved and celebrate success. This approach is more likely to encourage both learning risks and high expectations. Sometimes misdemeanours occur, these are much better dealt with in a calm, confident manner which says, *'I will see you at the end of the session'* or *'Come over here and let me have a quiet word with you'*, rather than announcing that everything is not well in the classroom.

9 Be punctual
A major lift in the achievement of schools could be secured if every teacher could agree to leave the staff room one minute before children were due in their classroom on every occasion for a year. The rise in 'productivity' would be amazing. Punctuality is one area where teachers really have to look at themselves and rigorously uphold expectations, not allowing personal time to overflow into professional time.

10 Being calm is easier said than done
Calmness occurs because of confidence, confidence arises from being sorted out, teachers are only sorted out when they have given a lot of thought to the logistics of the classroom and the learning experience they are planning.

11 Prepare children to listen to announcements
One source of disruption in classrooms is teachers who interrupt learning by making announcements. When children are engaged in lots of activities, visit groups to explain that in two minutes an announcement is to be made. The announcement should be made from the focal point *(see page 12)*. Since the teacher is making an announcement of some importance, it is reasonable to expect children to stop what they are doing, put down whatever they are holding and look and listen. Looking is as important as listening. By visiting groups rather than calling for quiet, stress is reduced and children realise that the teacher is controlling the classroom and enabling learning to take place. Visiting working groups simply prepares children to listen.

12 Ending the session
The ends of sessions in classrooms can be either enjoyable experiences or chaos. So much effort goes into planning a piece of teaching and organising it while it is taking place but often little thought goes into how it will end. This is one reason why children fail to understand what they have been doing, what they have learnt and why it was supposedly worthwhile, or the purpose of the work they were doing.

It is a common enough scene: children are engaged in an amazing number of different tasks and the clock is moving towards playtime. An announcement asks them to clear away. Different groups finish at different times, the noise level starts to rise and what was a comparatively quiet, calm classroom becomes a hive of activity of the clearing up variety and chaos ensues. Children's memories and impressions as they leave the classroom are of a less than happy learning experience and a less than satisfactory learning environment.

It would be much more enjoyable for everyone to stop the children with ten minutes to go, having visited all the groups, and to make it clear that they have been working well. Next, announce that over the next few minutes various groups are going to be asked to clear away and to suggest an order and a routine for clearing away and some reasons for that order. The clearing up should be timed and synchronised so that it all finishes together. This gives the opportunity on some occasions to use the last five minutes of the session to review what has been going on in the classroom, to look at:

- who has achieved what
- the different things people have been doing
- where people have been finding success
- where people have been taking risks
- the difficulties people have had
- the sort of help they need
- who might be the best person to help them.

This need not be the agenda for every session but it could happen a few times a week. On other occasions the teacher could use the time to test some tables or spellings, or who knows what is where on a map on the wall. In either case the session ends in a very different atmosphere from the session that drifts into oblivion and peters out.

13 Finishing off and getting started

Finishing off has so many meanings for children. The very notion of 'finishing' all your work says to children, 'that was the limit of expectation for this session or this week'. Putting up lists of work that the children have to do by a deadline, often constructs a self-defeating message: the list can look demanding, but for many children it represents a minimum set of objectives.

The Leeds Primary Needs Survey revealed how some children simply let time go by and work just before the deadline. *The Elton Report* talks about calculated idleness being one of the biggest causes of disruption in the classroom. Many children see a list of expectations and somehow seem able to calculate how long it will take to achieve them. They can therefore calculate how early they need to start before the deadline, and for some children a weekly list of work to be finished by Friday means that they only need to start on Thursday afternoon. From Monday until Thursday afternoon can be less than productive.

Many teachers find the 'getting started' period the most difficult when trying to operate a classroom that gives flexibility in learning. If getting started is so difficult, then the number of times that it is undertaken should be kept to a minimum. Finishing everything off by Friday means that Monday is a day of considerable stress. It is far easier to insist that children finish various pieces of work at different times but also to encourage *them* to work out what 'finished' really means and what would be suitable deadlines for completion.

Some ways to reduce problems of disruption in the classroom, given quality curriculum experiences

- Organise resources carefully and thoroughly *(see pages 14-18)*.
- Ensure clear 'traffic' areas *(see page 19)*.
- Give instructions, summarise, ask if anyone does not understand *(see pages 25-26, 48)*.
- Avoid queues, lines and crowds *(see pages 17 and 47)*.
- Avoid bribery and complex reward systems *(see pages 57-58)*.
- Avoid broadcasting 'concerns' and praise appropriate work behaviour *(see page 61)*.
- Praise in public, moan in private *(see page 61)*.
- Be punctual *(see page 61)*.
- Be calm *(see page 61)*.
- Prepare children to listen to 'announcements'; visit working groups rather than call for quiet *(see page 62)*.
- Pay special attention to the ends of sessions *(see page 62)*.
- Avoid 'finishing off' days; you only have to go through getting started once again *(see page 63)*.

Getting to know each other - laying foundations

The problem for teachers at the start of the year, with a new class, is that there are so many things to teach children, so many things for them to understand, and so many routines for them to get used to in a very short space of time. Teachers are torn between trying to communicate all the rules at once, with the obvious outcome that many are forgotten because they are not used, or trying to explain a ground rule after things have gone wrong. Overall ground rules need to be established, and then specific ones gradually set in place just before they are needed. There is little point in explaining any routine to children if it is not going to be practised immediately and reinforced. Planning should allow time early on for routines to be set, and later in the term for routines to be re-emphasised, not when they are going wrong but when they are going right, so that children appreciate the contribution they are making to the successful classroom.

To make children believe that they can achieve things and can reach high expectations, situations must be manipulated to ensure that children achieve success early. Children could be given short-term tasks early on in the term or just after a holiday. If these tasks use previous learning, they almost guarantee some success and build up levels of confidence. The level of challenge for children could be increased gradually rather than setting too much too early. It is important, though, not to give children tasks which are seemingly so trivial and obvious that they cannot really be bothered to do them properly.

Expecting children to act responsibly and explaining the systems is not enough, children need specific roles and jobs. They need to know exactly what is meant, and it is not realistic to think that children will correctly interpret generalised explanations of routines within the classroom.

- Time spent setting up systems is time well spent
- Explain systems gradually; not all at once but just before they are needed
- Try to achieve success early and give praise
- Expect children to act responsibly but give them 'specific' roles and jobs.

Time stealers and rigour losers

Registration

This can be as long or as short as you like. Registration has to be done, but how quickly can it be done and how much time can be saved for real learning? By making registration into an immediate activity the tone of the day can be established as children enter the classroom.

Need registration be done with nothing else going on besides? Is it beyond the scope of many children to work at their task as well as listen for their name? Must their name be called at all? Can it be established in some other way whether the children are there or not? Some nursery classrooms operate systems of self-registration that put secondary schools to shame. Little children are able to take charge of their own entry to the classroom and exercise real responsibility through clocking-in systems, charts, or checklists.

Collecting money

Many schools have systems for collecting dinner money these days which takes the burden of administration away from teachers. Yet collecting money is a constant source of irritation and takes time away from teaching and learning. Money collection can be a real opportunity for children to count actual cash and to keep records. In some classrooms collecting money can be quick, efficient and worthwhile, in other classrooms it can be slow, laborious and detrimental.

Getting equipment

In some classrooms it takes children a considerable time to collect their equipment and to get themselves organised. In other classrooms children are ready because their equipment is organised and well managed. The teacher has a responsibility to ensure that the overall framework is clear and understood by everybody. The children have a responsibility not only for getting equipment out but also for putting it back in the right place every time. Children should be encouraged to be quick to get out equipment and they should get the right equipment for the task.

When working with the whole class, the teacher can act as the distributor of resources rather than expecting every child to leave their seat and fetch what they need. This means that efficient techniques for distribution, understood by everyone, are used consistently. Habits such as placing a set of papers on a table for the group rather than handing a piece to each child are obvious time-savers.

Changing

One form of equipment that can take time to organise is specialist clothing for PE, games or swimming. Children need to learn how to change, how to fetch their clothes and how to organise their clothing so that when they return they can quickly change back into everyday wear. Just as with other routines, getting changed needs to be practised. If it is practised and if emphasis is placed on saving time children will respond. If the emphasis is on doing things over and over again in order to do them properly children will respond by becoming slower.

Teachers being late

To promote rigorous work behaviour and achievement in the classroom, one of the most significant steps is to be there when the children come in and to start on time. There is nothing more potent in setting expectations than being there.

Fridays, Mondays, wet days, windy days, hot days, days before holidays and first days of term

It is easy to say that some days are not worth using and to find a rationalisation for failure to achieve things. Fridays cannot be sacrificed to clearing up and finishing off, otherwise the belief is instilled in children that Fridays are not important and do not matter too much. Everybody has off days in teaching and in learning. The important thing is to ensure that these days are kept to a minimum and do not become an excuse for a lack of rigour.

Wet days are different. Teachers know that they are going to be different, and should organise the time differently so that children get a balance of activity and demand through the day, and vary their tasks not just between subjects but between the way in which the subjects are approached.

Sometimes it is useful to think carefully about what is taken for granted within the classroom. Many teachers wring their hands and expect wet days to be a problem, and regard them with dread. Perhaps it is worth going back to basics and considering:

- Do children need a playtime if they cannot go out to play?
- Can they have small table/group visits to toilets?
- Keep wet day games in a special storage place.
- Wet day games away, ready to start work at the right time.
- Predict the day, plan the pattern.

Then announce it, and enjoy it!

In all honesty, playtime is not for the children's benefit but for that of the grown-ups in the school. Is the benefit from having 'our playtime' worthwhile considering the tensions sometimes created by what goes on immediately afterwards?

Some schools no longer have playtimes on wet days. This is very sensible since wet days do not allow play to take place. The teachers recognise that the day is going to be difficult, that everybody is going to be in all day, and they try to plan the types of work that the children will be engaged in. There will be times when the children are active, other times when they are passive; they do work which is novel and new, but also things that they enjoy and are good at. Teachers take a break when it is appropriate and will have a cup of coffee as and when they can, perhaps leaving a well-briefed adult with the children. This is far better than all the teachers leaving their classrooms at once, leaving one teacher to patrol or, perhaps worse, some older children as vigilantes.

Behaviour: the child's view

Children's insights are fascinating. Intuitively, they know so much about classrooms and understand how they operate. Some children were asked to fill in a questionnaire about behaviour. A selection of their thought-provoking, and frequently amusing, comments is given on pages 67-70. You might like to use them with your own class. Discovering what children think and feel can only result in more sensitive, thoughtful teaching. As you read through the children's responses try to work out what the children see as appropriate and inappropriate behaviour and, more importantly, how they have got these messages. The children do not use terms like Talking Out Of Turn, Hindering Other Children, Out Of Seat, or Non-Verbal Noise - but they know an awful lot about them.

Think again about your responses to the children's answers:

- What can be learnt about the way classrooms are organised from the views of these children?
- What messages come through about the importance of relevance and purpose in the curriculum?
- What could teachers do to take some of the tensions out of the classroom for children?
- What aspects of organisation in classrooms come shining through as areas to be addressed?

Think about times when you have misbehaved in school recently. What sort of misbehaviour have you done?

I have made a littel noise when the teacher has Just nipped out for a few minutes.

If all the children in your class lined up starting with the best behaved going back to the worst, where would you stand?
Put a cross:

Best — Worst

Think about times when you have misbehaved in school recently. What sort of misbehaviour have you done?

I have been misbehaving by running around the class for noreeson.

I have puched to get first in the line once. And I have been writing whille the teching is talking.

on fridays I get silly and messaboute.

Think about your worst behaviour this year. What was it and what made it bad?

not enaf werk and geting told off.

warsting card !!!!

What sort of bad behaviour by other children annoys you?

in the Hall when peple in essembly slap
ther hym books down.

It's burping.

What can your teachers do to help your behaviour be as good as possible?

not as much riting.

More of a challenge

being in a friendly classroom
and having interesting lessons.

ART

standing in the corner would because
it makes your legs feel weary.

What sorts of things would make you behave better?

more exciting lessons
to stop spellings
make school a bit fairer

ask me if I want to do my own thing for a change

I don't think they can do anything.

10 *Homework*

Traditionally, homework has not been a widespread feature of primary schools. Apart from giving children a weekly list of spellings or tables to learn, the nearest most schools have got to homework is the suggestion that children could 'follow things up' at home. Children might be asked to see what they can find out about something, or whether they have any objects at home that link with a topic, but the level of expectation on the part of children and teachers has been limited, with no regular commitment on the part of home or school.

In recent years some schools have started to develop the idea of providing children with work to do at home. This is partly to do with extending the long-held view that children do better when the school and home work in partnership. It is partly to do with responding to requests from some parents and partly to do with trying to offer a consistent programme for children rather than the hit-or-miss, sporadic programme that occurs in most schools, where homework can be set on some occasions but not others, or forgotten, or appear out of the blue without any discernible pattern.

There are several reasons why offering homework makes sense:

1 Some children like to continue school work at home
2 Links are made with home
3 Parent demand is kept 'in proportion'
4 A 'routine' commitment is set
5 Parents are offered a way of helping their child
6 Children's personal interests are built upon
7 Another picture for assessment is available

If homework has its advantages then it is worthwhile for teachers to consider the possibilities. The problem is that the homework can get out of hand, start to 'run' the teacher, and become a self-defeating system. In order to maintain control the teacher needs to set a programme which is manageable for all concerned. Rather than a routine set of homework tasks it is possible to include homework activities in the planning of work for each term. Because the homework is planned 'up front' the pressure upon the teacher is reduced, a range of tasks is provided, one piece of homework links to another, and the work complements that planned for the classroom.

In the example of a homework programme for a Year 3 class on page 72 it is possible to see a variety of activities for the child all linked to the overall plan for the term. If children are going to do homework they 'sign up' for the programme and their parents also sign to say

Homework programme - audiences Spring Term

Week ending

13 January	Learn words for individual roles and class assembly.
20 January	Make a list of safety warnings and things which are dangerous to explain to the class - link to module one sign making.
27 January	Prepare a book review to present during a library session - emphasis on story beginnings.
10 February	Prepare questions for interviews for roles in a 'film production' of Snow White within the year group, to set up interviews for: cameraman director producer costume department.
16 February	Write letters to inform successful candidates that they have got the above jobs.
28 February	Review three scripts written within the year group for clarity of layout so that each actor will be clear what they have to say.
10 March	Prepare a five minute talk on a subject of interest to present to the class. Inclusion of props. Three weeks to complete.
31 March	Review and critical analysis of their talk to the class - what they would change? How they would improve their talk/use of props?
7 April	Collect objects for next term's theme - wheels, books about space, toys which move in different ways.

they will offer support and encourage the children to fulfil their commitment. The following term the children decide whether they will sign up again. Since the programme is optional, the children can take part or not, depending upon their other out-of-school commitments, but they are not committing themselves for ever, just one term.

Periodically, children are provided with support or advice sheets *(see below)* on the tasks set, to help them and their parents. These sheets serve to remind children and parents of the commitment and to keep the programme on schedule. The sheets are prepared at the planning stage, along with the other activities for the term.

Your homework for March

1 Think about **something you are really interested in**.
Something that makes you feel excited.
Something you can't wait to do.

2 Think about **a person** you would like to share it with.
It could be a friend, a teacher, your Mum and Dad, your grandparents, the lunch lady or anyone else you know.

3 Now think **how you would tell them** all about it in five minutes.
Would you just talk to them?
Show them some photographs?
Make a poster or a model?
Share some work you have done?

4 **Practice your talk.**
Ask your family to listen to you.
Can they hear you?
Are your words clear?
Are you making them feel interested?

Such systems, once established, have values which will help learning:

- Decisions are placed with the child
- Deadlines are set
- Children can organise their own time
- Different levels of work are allowed for
- A range of work styles is offered
- Ritual work is avoided
- Partnered projects are possible.

A homework programme thus becomes a powerful opportunity to develop classroom work for children. The advantages given above are significant features of good classroom practice. A good homework programme extends good classroom practice without becoming a burden to children or teachers.

11 *Reviewing with children*

An aspect of classroom life that is often overlooked is the need to review work with children. Involving children in their learning, giving them purposes and reasons, and the importance of processes in learning is often talked about. Yet so often children come to the end of the task and that is it, finished. It might be marked, displayed or read out, all of which give a response and recognise success, but does this go far enough in giving children a picture of how their learning is developing? Engaging children in a planned review of their work fulfils several functions. If time is regularly put aside for review, the gains will be apparent as they become used to the process and routines.

Recognise success and progress
When people go on a journey they prefer to know where they are going. Sometimes the thought of the ground to be covered can be daunting and they feel better if they stop for a while and look at what has been accomplished already. So it is with strugglers in classrooms. Often strugglers move through each level, they become convinced that they cannot do anything. They need to stop, look at where they started and at what they have achieved. This is one reason why record keeping is important. As well as giving teachers a picture of development, the child can see the progress made, which is often more than the child realises.

Help children look back at learning
Seeing where the learning went and following the progress of a piece of work is important in all subjects. If the whole picture is not seen, then each task becomes an isolated activity unconnected to the overall challenge, production or performance. Whether it is in art, English, PE or mathematics, it is important for children to be able to reflect on the process in which they have been involved.

The example on page 75 comes from a five-year-old who has been doing some science involving making paint from soil. There are obvious links with art and history but the main purpose of the activity was the science. As the child worked through the investigation, she wrote her thoughts on separate pieces of paper and these were put together at the end with her picture to show the thinking behind it. By working on the thinking, the teacher can help the child to look back on the learning. The danger of simply displaying the soil painting would be that the emphasis might be on the art rather than on the aspects of learning that were important.

MY INVESTIGATION

TITLE Soil Paint

THE TASK

T We have to find out Which soil will mace the Best Paint

I THINK

? I think Clay soil WILL Be Win Becuses it is Sticky

OTHER THINGS TO THINK ABOUT

We need 30g of ethe soil

I NEED

N Water

put the Same amant of water in

WHAT I DID

D first I put 30g of soil in a tuB and put 30g of water in

WHAT HAPPENED

H We maDe Paint

WHAT I FOUND OUT

F the Rith soil was the Best Becse it is dark

IF I DID THIS AGAIN I WOULD

Q I woue put more soil in

Children of all ages need help to realise the point of what they have been doing. Learning can be interesting and fun but the teacher has to make sure that the children know why they are doing the tasks set. Children should realise that they are doing mathematics when they play with plastic or that they are learning history when they go on a visit to the museum. By encouraging this child to review her soil painting the teacher has a chance to emphasise the scientific processes.

Value effort

Children need to be able to say that they have worked hard and put in a lot of effort. So often comments about these things come from other people. Teachers tell children that they have tried hard and done well. Sometimes they tell them that more effort is needed. It is right that they should. It is also right that children should be aware of how much effort they have put in, whether they have really tried and whether their work is the best they can do. Effective review with children will help them to value their own efforts.

Identify difficulties

If difficulties are identified, there is a chance to do something about them. Using review to highlight problems can be good for children and teachers.

Today has been ~~one of~~ the werst day back at school So for this term. I've watched other people do it and I've Never thorght it would happen to me.

You have really made a mess with the football Neil. You <u>must</u> have kicked it <u>very</u> hard indeed you know. It should <u>not</u> have broken the glass. Football is for the <u>pitch</u>, once you are over the line it is out of bounds!

Look at children's perceptions

Children's views of learning are often interesting, sometimes illuminating, thought-provoking and challenging. Their views can form a basis for action on the part of the teacher. The examples below come from learning logs kept by children, in which they record their thoughts about their learning on a regular basis. In some cases the teacher responds but in others the children's record acts as a focus for their impressions of classroom life and learning. The act of reflecting on and reviewing learning is one that will happen anyway. Teachers have much to gain by knowing what children think and by trying to help them as they look back.

today has been O.K. can we do more pattern tilés tomomow? why coudent we do maths today?. I think that I have worked bad today Kem talking. will you stop pileing the hand-writing on me? Bye.

What do you mean, stop piling the handwriting on you? If you need to practice handwriting you do need to do it!

I did not understand anything before I came to ST Johns but now I can understand things that I have not been taught yet.

12 *Classroom management and organisation*

Here is a checklist that you may find useful in reviewing your own classroom organisation.

In preparation for teaching do you:

1 Gather resources before lessons begin?
2 Prepare the classroom for the next lesson
- before school?
- through playtime?
- through lunchtime?
- at the end of the day for the next day?

3 Hold a plan in mind for the rhythm of the day?
4 Tell the children in advance what to do next?
5 Insist that all work is finished before starting new work?
6 Provide on-going tasks in the classroom?
7 Provide 'more of the same' for extension tasks?
8 Provide a rich day for learning which is:
- challenging enough?
- supportive enough?

9 Note how much of your planning has been achieved each day?
10 Change the plan for the next day in the light of today's work?

In preparation for learning do you:

1 Leave your space clear and tidy at the end of each day?
2 Insist children leave their classroom tidy at the end of the day?
3 Ensure corridors and workbays are tidy before going home?
4 Provide a labelled place for everything to be stored?
5 Teach children to put things back where they came from?
6 Have uniform storage systems for curriculum areas?
7 Clear finished work off boards each day?
8 Clear computer disks into wallets at the end of each session?
9 Ensure sink areas are clean and tidy daily?
10 Pick up the debris of the day in the cloakroom?

For professional time management do you:

1 Ensure phone calls are returned or made before going home?
2 See any parents you wanted to see as soon as possible?
3 Make any appointments that need making with:
- parents?
- staff?
- outside agencies?

4 Record any observations on the day they occur?
5 Send memos, letters, information when requested?

As manager of your environment do you:

1 Ensure tidy trays are tidied and appropriately equipped?
2 Check that the paper trolley has enough pre-cut paper?
3 Keep an eye on watering and repotting plants?
4 Wash aprons regularly?
5 Top up powder paint systems?
6 Sharpen pencils in advance?
7 Weed out broken equipment regularly?
8 Check the state of books, dictionaries, word banks?
9 Empty cupboards, drawers and behind curtains regularly?
10 Ask the children what they think needs doing or improving?

Standing back - asking questions

What is the teacher doing?
- demanding?
- supervising?
- observing?
- teaching?

What sort of work is seen?
- all subjects?
- skills?
- approaches?
- reasons?

How hard are they working?
- effort?
- purpose?
- speed?

Who is doing what:
- levels of work?
- groupings/tasks?
- with the teacher?

How well are they working?
- speed?
- product?
- ideas?

What qualities are seen in the children?
- responsibility?
- decision making?
- consideration?
- politeness?

What impression does the room give?
- fuss?
- tidiness?
- organisation?
- display?

Index